THE CAPITAL OF PARADISE

A MEMOIR

MARK A. TAYLOR

OXIDE BOOKS

Scottsdale, Arizona

ISBN 978-0-9818930-2-0

This is a Juniper Press and Oxide Books product,
Published by Juniper Press

Book/Cover Design: Rachel Scott

Printed and distributed in the United States

Library of Congress Cataloging-In-Publication Data

Taylor, Mark A. 1949 –
A Memoir: The Capital of Paradise

OTHER BOOKS BY MARK A. TAYLOR

Patriots: The Redrock Land War
A Novel
Oxide Books and Juniper Press 2008

Sandstone Sunsets
Non-fiction – Journey to Self Enlightenment
Gibb Smith Books – 1998

Wild and Beautiful
A collection of naturalist essays
Gibb Smith Books – 1999

Chaco: A Tale of Ancient Lives
Novel
Sunstone Press
Santa Fe, New Mexico – 1994

ACKNOWLEDGEMENTS

At the Round Table:
Randall Potts, Nancy Alvey, Sylvia Knight, Mick Tripp,
Robin Johnson, Wendy Wood, Bud Mixon, Leslie Majors
and Iris Santos.

Life Companions
Basker the Boy, Scout Master, Tsar, Grace Taylor, Lilmum
Taylor, Whitestuff, Ava Taylor, Saint Taylor.

Special Thanks
Ron Godfrey
Stephanie Young Merzel
Grant Bassett

DEDICATION: WITH ALL MY LOVE

Lana Mitchell
Lonnie Burton
Margo Taylor

CHAPTER ONE

APRIL 2017

RIO VERDE, ARIZONA

"Talk to Ben?" Lana asks.

"No."

"Think you should?"

Lana and I are on the patio enjoying a glass of wine after dinner. This time of year the Sonoran desert is sumptuous. Saguaro, oleander, oxatillo and bougainvillea are in bloom and exotic fragrances float in and out on the evening air. A bird of prey glides across the gold and blue light. Sunset, silence and solitude blend and create a lacuna or separate reality that only nature can produce.

"Ben has nothing to do with this...he's in Clearwater. I'm working for Hollywood."

Touching her wine glass to her bottom lip Lana continues, "Is there someone you can talk to?"

"Don't want to talk to anyone, baby."

"But you said yourself 'this project is designed to fail.'"

"Indeed - it is and it will."

"What about Bill?"

Lana is worried about my mental state and health. I'm pushing hard and haven't had a day off since mid-October.

"Bill?" I scoff.

"Miscavige's lawyer."

"Oh, Bill Walsh! No, no - he's pushing the deadlines."

Fed-Ex just wheeled away from my studio after delivering more boxes of confidential church documents including secret investigative reports, legal affidavits, executive memoranda and reference books from the Scientologists' legal archives. All totaled they could weigh forty pounds. This is the third installment and I hope the last. Most are original or one-of-a-kind documents dealing with the sixty-year battle between the church, the American Psychiatric Association, the CIA and federal law enforcement agencies. I'm hoping this delivery might contain answers to the niggling questions I've run up against and provide me with the missing link evidence essential to make an unassailable case.

This project has fascinating facets and over the years I've been drawn to or sought out the unusual or strange high value freelance or contract assignments. Unlike journalists who get an education, place a few stories here and there with magazines and newspapers until they land a conventional job and stable paycheck, I work for myself, picking subjects and topics that intrigue me – despite the stress and grinding economic hardship that sometimes go along with it. It's one of those trade-offs writers and artists make with the hope it will work out.

I spent a year writing about the Hopi/Navajo land relocation act because I love the land and respect Native American reverence for it. For a two-year period I wrote about suicide after my best friend Mick took his life. I stopped when I realized no matter how hard I worked I couldn't bring him back or soothe my sorrow. Mick's death and that of others shattered my dream into shards of colored glass and in some inexplicable way altered my life's trajectory one splinter at a time. Eventually, I turned inward and was consumed with visions of empty boats, bone-white moons and the waves and walls of time.

I'm particularly interested in mysteries with no solution. This fascination has taken me to hobo jungles and rail yards where I catch-out on midnight freight trains in open boxcars. I've disappeared into the vast sandstone canyon deserts of southern Utah in search of a lost poet (Everett Ruess) and the source of humanity's unfulfilled dreams. I've traveled all four directions and explored the fifth – the perpendicular one that goes from the outside of us to the inside. I've written books and essays about such obtuse things. In the meantime, I scratched out a living as a naturalist writer, an art magazine publisher, book editor, ghost-writer, instructor of creative nonfiction writing and an investigative journalist.

And now I've come full circle. Once upon a time I sold blockbuster expose' about Kip Eliason and Jimmy Swaggart to major markets, while condemning religious hypocrisy and unmasking its charlatan leaders. Eliason was a beautiful sixteen-year-old Mormon boy who committed suicide over his inability to stop masturbating. I went undercover to infiltrate Jimmy Swaggart's Assemblies of God congregation and discovered his asinine peccadillos and numerous fraudulent enterprises. And today I toil in the vineyard of the religious faithful where I have perfected the narrative voice of God – a voice so sweet it erases the bardo between transcendental insight and the direct experience of existential reality.

All of which brings me back to today's Fed-Ex delivery. A writer's life is a circuitous path and this time around I've traded my hard-won freelance persona for a six-figure salary, an at-will employee agreement, and a chance to stick my finger in the eye of the profession of psychiatry and the Central Intelligence Agency. For the temporary inconvenience of being employed, I get a prestigious book contract and a free pass into the inner-sanctum of perhaps America's most secretive and fascinating churches – the Scientologists.

Early the next morning, Lana and I, along with Ava and Pierre our pups, head out from the house on foot for a hike in the Sonoran desert. We live just a few hundred yards from the forty-thousand acre McDowell Mountain Nature reserve and a little used trailhead leading into one of its most remote areas.

The trail heads west and follows a wide flood plain covered in fairy duster bushes, crown of thorn and beehive cacti and oxatillo and mesquite trees. Eventually, we enter a hidden valley between two hills where the land is populated by giant saguaro cactus standing on either hillside. Some of these giants are fifty feet tall and have the presence of royal personages. We call this place the Valley of the Giants and their arms reach skyward in an uplifting joyous gesture. It's easy to see the saguaro as dancers celebrating life and its magnificence. Our moods are always buoyed in this natural place.

Resting in the shade of a particularly fat Saguaro we spot a Harrington hawk in a nearby tree. Unlike the vast pink and bronze sandstone canyon country of southern Utah and the high Colorado Plateau where I spent a lifetime exploring and writing, the Sonoran desert is lush and filled with exotic plants and animal life.

A little further along we hike the backbone of one ridge after another and I realize I've been living in or been consumed by one desert landscape or another – real or metaphorical – most of my life. I was raised in an intellectual desert and cultural wasteland created by elements of the Mormon Church. They find disdain and distrust in everything considered "worldly". If you are not a member of the church, Utah is a desolate, unwelcoming and lonely place.

The Mormons settled an equal distance from Denver and San Francisco so they could be alone to develop its own brand of austere dogma. Secretly, many in the church scorn outsiders and everything they represent. Like Goldmond from Hermann Hesse's book, *Narcissus and Goldmond*, I struck out early and discovered southern Utah and the greatest contemplative landscape on the planet. And today I live at the northern end of the Sonoran desert and I can feel this place is in my DNA.

My old friend and distinguished professor of Shakespeare and American Literature, Phil Sullivan, once asked me, "Have you ever noticed how great art and civilizations get their start near great oceans and waterways? And how important spiritual enterprises and religions spring from hot and unforgiving deserts?"

RIO VERDE

MAY 2017

It's been another difficult week. A mysterious energy loss hounds me and its accompanying back pain will not relent. If I weren't working a tight deadline I might take a break, but I need to push forward. I'm glad the work is fascinating and keeps me at my desk.

This chapter of *The Attacks on Scientology* book is a big and unwieldy piece that starts in the present then flashes back to the 1920s and before the battle waged by the psychiatric community for acceptance and credibility within the larger medical world. Modern medicine is based on verifiable, data-driven scientific evidence, while psychiatry in most cases, cannot offer these same result-oriented metrics.

Each generation of psychiatrists produces a new crop of charlatans and fakers who push outlandish cures and treatments on unsuspecting patients. Even today, many in the medical community consider psychiatry to be a breeding ground for ludicrous and inhumane treatments.

The second half of this chapter focuses on L. Ron Hubbard and his wildly successful self-help technology, Dianetics, and his clash with the psychiatric community after its publication. Released in 1950, *Dianetics: The Modern Science of Mental Health* remained on the New York Times bestseller list for 28 weeks. Newspapers called Dianetics the fastest-growing movement in America. This success and media attention focused the ire of American Psychiatric Association to go on attack. It claimed the technology of Dianetics was suspect and simply did not work, and further it alleged that L. Ron Hubbard was an imposter. Psychiatry saw Hubbard and Dianetics as threats to its influence and a competing treatment it could not control or subsume. Hubbard responded with claims that Dianetics had helped tens of thousands of people, and with charges that since the conclusion of WWII, psychiatry and the CIA were involved in secret and deadly mind control experiments on unwitting American citizens. These charges and counter charges ushered in a tit-for-tat battle fought out in courts and in the public opinion arena. This battle is now in its sixth decade.

In my view, many of the principles of Dianetics work and help some people face problems and challenges in a constructive and positive way. I have worked with church executives on and off for a decade and without exception found them to be clear-headed truth-tellers whose competitive zeal can get in the way. They face problems with a sober and solution-oriented style. They demand eye contact and are present in the moment. Most are Type A personalities and intensely aggressive in the way of high achievers.

Because of my work for the Scientologists I am occasionally asked if I'm a member of the church. I respond in short declarative sentences: "I am not a Scientologist. I have never been a Scientologist. I will never be a Scientologist." In my case, I have never had more than an anthropological or passing interest in monotheistic belief systems. I have no interest in pursuing the invisible magic man who lives in the sky. For me, ultimately, I ascribe to what Albert Einstein said in his famous 1954 God Letter. He wrote, "The word God is for me nothing but the expression and product of human weaknesses, the Bible a collection of venerable but still rather primitive legends. "

Notwithstanding, Dianetics may be the best self-help technology ever developed; but in my view it should have never morphed into an organized religion. Part of the reason it happened as it did was timing. In 1950, shortly after WWII, tens of thousands were lost and looking for help outside the traditional religious institutions that had failed them. They were what author Gertrude Stein called, "a lost generation" searching for a way to move forward after the devastation of a terrible war. Dianetics seemed to fit this need. It also made sense given so many people found initial and dramatic benefit from the technology and methods it offered.

ROUND TABLE ONE

Late that night after Lana and the pups are in bed, I slip out onto the patio and sit in the darkness and silence. Nighttime has always held a mystic power and tonight the Milky Way stretches from horizon to horizon and casts a soft misty glow across the desert floor. Somewhere coyotes are singing a wild and mournful song. For the last few months I've fought a terrible fatigue and a deep gnawing weakness radiating out from my center. Something is wrong and I'm fearful of what it might be. My joints ache and my ankles, knees, hips and wrists are weak and numb.

My thoughts drift and float to my friend Mick Tripp and how after he died I discovered he was still alive inside my head. Years have come and gone and tonight I'm transported back again to that fateful night along the Colorado River.

After leaving Moab, I drive east along the river road and camp on the wide sandy beach at a place called Big Bend. I know this spot well and have base-camped here many times while exploring Canyonlands and Arches National Parks.

In the late 1960s, Big Bend was little known and locals called it Nude Beach. I often camped there with other bohemian sun worshipers who had found their way to its sandy beaches from places the world over. Hidden from the roadway, we swam, sunbathed, and celebrated the silence. At night we stood naked around campfires and talked in whispers. It mattered little that we did not know one another; our golden nakedness assured us we were of the same tribe.

Over the years, I have come to enjoy arriving in the sandstone canyons after dark, and this particular night was no exception. I bailed out of my car, filled my lungs with clean air, pushed my hands into the small of my back, and arced to look at the Milky Way. Wow! Viewing the stars from the desert never fails to astound me.

Somewhere in the darkness, the Colorado River washes against its shoreline. The river calls out to me, reminding me that I stood in the exact place where years earlier my best friend, Mick Tripp, told me he loved me. I look down, hoping to see his footprints lying there in the dirt, but they are long gone. Instead, my eyes follow the well-worn path to a small grove of gambel oak trees where I normally camp. Since my feet know the path so well, I let them carry me to the oaks, then through an opening in a line of thick tamarisk trees and down to the river.

At the river's edge, I stand and face upstream and then downstream. Starlight reflects off the water's surface making it appear placid and inviting, yet its roiling undertow frightens me and I feel insignificant standing next to it. Not wanting to parade my intimidation, I plop down in the sand and sit Indian style. I was the only human being for miles and not entirely welcomed by the river.

Just one month before Mick killed himself with a bullet to his heart, he and I escaped Salt Lake City and ran south into the desert. We camped at Big Bend and hiked the canyons. We hiked fast without stopping to rest, searching every alcove and hidden draw, every slope and amphitheater. We dropped stones into canyons and climbed escarpments. We were searching for something but had no idea what it was.

During a cavalier moment as Mick and I stood surveying a fine prospect of sandstone formations, I told him that the face of every man, woman and child who has ever lived can be found in the sandstone cliffs and formations.

"If that is so," he said, "then, I too, shall one day reside here."

Since Mick's death, I have seen him here three times. The first time, I was watching a magnificent sunset above Arch Canyon when out on the serrated horizon, the silhouette of his face appeared. It was perfect to a minute detail. The next time, I was atop Grandview Point in Canyonlands when his face took shape in the morning shadow of Junction Butte below me, moving across an expanse of sagebrush flats until it twisted, contorted, and became unrecognizable. The last time I saw Mick's face, it was rendered on a palette of rain-soaked, vermillion-colored Kayenta sandstone above Davis Gulch where Everett Ruess disappeared.

From the beach, I search the surrounding cliffs, hoping the starlight might catch Mick there. He is out there somewhere, I told myself, along with all the others – but tonight they remain hidden.

I become restless sitting on the beach, so I move to the grove of gambel oaks where Mick unrolled his sleeping bag for the very last time. The night was liquid and I couldn't shake my fear of the river. I was convinced Mick wanted to live. Standing next to some nearby rocks, he told me of his plan to buy a new Harley Davidson motorcycle.

On his last night in the desert, Mick sat against the very tree trunk where I now sit.

"Life and death come face to face in the desert," he told me. "Our lives have little consequence in view of the 300 million years of history around us here. When I am gone my friend, this is where you will find me."

It has been five years since Mick took his leave, and I honor him more with each passing season. Strange as it may sound, I have kept my friend alive by incorporating his voice and point of view into the world of my internal dialogues. He now advocates at the round table of my soul, speaking to me if he has something to say, and if I query him, he is always there to answer.

"Hey Mick!" I shouted out into the unattached darkness, "What am I lookin' at on the other side, Bro?"

From the cold river below came his reply, "Taylor, the

only thing waiting for you is an icy black river of night!"

There was a moment of silence, and then he cut loose with his famous horselaugh, the one I hated when he was alive.

He is here with me tonight in Rio, advocating from his seat at the round table of my internal dialogues. He speaks to me if he has something to say and if I query him, he is always there to answer. Mick is not the only one at the round table. There are others – people I have loved and lost – and they occupy seats as well. They now sit cheek-by-jowl at the table of my soulful deliberations.

I move out away from the house and the Palo Verde trees. At the center of some open space I tilt my face sky-ward into the center of the Milky Way.

"Mick!" I holler out, "What say you?"

CHAPTER TWO

RIO VERDE

Received an email from Gene Eliason telling me about a teenaged girl being held against her will in a basement on the east side of Salt Lake City in an upscale neighborhood by her uncle, the leader of one of the many fundamentalist Mormon cults that marble the body of the larger church in the valley.

I haven't heard from Eliason in a long time. Years earlier, I helped him gain national attention and a sense of justice for the death of his son, Kip Eliason. Kip took his life after battling the "terrible addiction" and sin of masturbation as mandated by his beloved Mormon Church. At the time, Church President Spencer Kimball wrote that premarital sex, petting and masturbation were stepping-stones to mental illness and suicide.

Kip Eliason was a beautiful, smart, athletic Mormon boy who loved the church. His mother died early and his father wasn't prepared to raise him so he lived with his grandmother. Kip was devoted to the church and Gene felt the church served as a second mother and even father to him. Kip took the church teachings seriously and when as a teenager he started having sexual urges and began masturbating, he became depressed and despondent. The church rules are clear, masturbation is a sin and he couldn't be a righteous Mormon unless he stopped this disgusting practice. He felt a great responsibility to live up to the chruch's teachings. At church services, teachers and the bishop often asked Kip to stand and used him as an example to young boys of everything a young man should aspire too.

Kip was living a lie and betraying God and his church. He spent more and more time alone, reading scriptures and the speeches from church authorities, even underlining sections about sin and sex. After his death, his father Gene discovered a 246 pages handwritten journal outlining his two-year battle to stop masturbating and expressing the self-loathing and hatred he felt for himself. There were copies of speeches from church leadership talking about the sin of sex before marriage and the irreparable damage done to the soul of offenders. In his suicide letter addressed to his father he wrote, "Go on with your life, I would rather die and live in hell forever than be burdened by this unforgivable sin of masturbation. "

When Kip confessed his sin to his bishop, he was admonished to stop and told of the negative consequence to his church membership if he didn't. The approach was punitive and he was labeled deviant. He was given a booklet entitled, "18 Way to Overcome Masturbation," which reads like a medieval anti-sex screed. It advises masturbators to wear extra layers of clothing when in bed so your penis is harder to access; to never be alone especially in the bathroom; and to tie the hand one masturbates with to a bed frame.

Unlike churches that require priests or clergy to have a formal education or bachelor's degree in religious counseling, the Mormon faith relies on untrained and part-time volunteer elders called bishops to oversee its wards or congregations. Kip's bishop managed an automobile quick lube business, had a high school education and could not identify mental illness or know how to treat it. After Kip's confession this bishop went to the University of Utah bookstore and purchased a number of behavioral modification therapy textbooks used by licensed psychologists and psychiatrists and implemented his own version of sex therapy on Kip.

When Kip attempted suicide and doctors learned of

the unlicensed counseling, they warned church leaders of its danger and demanded it cease such counseling. Gene told his son that all young people, both boys and girls, masturbate and it was healthy and normal. But Kip would have none of it, saying it may be fine for others, but not for him.

After his death, Eliason filed a 26 million dollar clergy malpractice suit against the Church of Latter Day Saints charging its beliefs or dogma was responsible for Kip's suicide. Further, the suit charged church authorities counseled Kip and instituted dangerous behavior modification therapies without training, psychological degrees or licensing. It claimed these actions first rendered him suicidal and ultimately led him to commit the act.

Kip's death set Gene off on a crusade to expose the Mormon churches view/treatment of the normal and healthy sexual development of children and subsequently, the sex crimes against girls and young women in the patriarchal religion.

Eliason's email said the girl had repeatedly tried to leave her fundamentalist church after her father died in an industrial accident and her mother promised the thirteen-year-old in marriage to her father's brother. The girl escaped twice but was returned to the abusive and sexually explosive situation by the Salt Lake City Police Department.

I first met Gene Eliason when I had an office at the Marmalade Hill Center, an old onion-domed Russian Orthodox church converted into a theater space on the west side of the historic Capital hill. It was a sweet office that I renovated and I spent my time writing proposals, pitching stories, taking assignments from local and regional publications and working on a novel.

Gene had read an investigative cover story I generated for Utah Holiday Magazine, titled, *The Love That Dare Not Speak Its Name*, about Utah's gay community, the AIDS epidemic, and a local entrepreneur, Babs DeLay's outing of Pam Parsons, the head coach of the women's National Championship Women's Collegiate Basketball Team at South Carolina, for sexual assault and intimidation of women basketball players in her program. The story was picked up by United Press International and gained some national attention, but it was another piece, an essay about my friend, Mick Tripp, and his suicide that made the elder Eliason pick up the phone and call me. He said he needed a writer who knew something about pain and suicide.

On our first meeting Gene Eliason arrived at my office as I sat on the steps outside talking with Nancy Borgenicht, the artistic director of the Salt Lake Acting Company. He reminded me of Robert Redford as the Sundance Kid. He was handsome, mustached and he wore a tan sport coat, Levis and cowboy boots. He was soft spoken and after introductions we went inside to my office.

He showed me family photographs and letters Kip had written. He had school certificates of accomplishment and copies of speeches and excerpts from church general authorities that he found after Kip's death in his journal. Gene felt guilty and responsible for what happened and for letting Kip sink so far that he took his life.

He then passed an envelope across the desk to me. It was addressed to him and had a splashy Playboy Magazine logo and return address. The letter was from Hugh Hefner and introduced a Playboy writer assigned to generate Kip's story. Hefner was excited to share/exploit Kip's tragic story with his audience and said the writer was nationally known, trusted and had worked on important projects for him.

"I met her last week," Eliason said. "She flew out and it didn't work out."

"What happened?" I asked.

Pushing back in his seat he gazed at the ceiling, "Honestly, there was something phony about her and I didn't like it." He took a deep breath, "She wouldn't listen either, and had ideas about telling Kip's story without knowing a damn thing about him."

"I see," I shifted from bun to bun. Just a week earlier, Robert Gottlieb, Editor-In-Chief of the New Yorker Magazine turned down a chapter excerpt from my unpublished book, *Sandstone Sunsets*. It was a real disappointment, but now with no effort on my part a new opportunity was knocking at my door.

I contacted the New Yorker, The Atlantic and New Republic magazines. There was great interest in Kip's story, especially the possible precedent setting aspect of clergy malpractice. If the suit prevailed, it would be the first time in American jurisprudence that an established religion would be held legally responsible for the wrongful death of a member because of its teachings or dogma. The problem was, these editorial publications did not have the endless resources – if required - to fight a protracted legal battle against a major American religion.

The sexual aspect of the story was spectacular, inflammatory and problematic as well. At the time the political climate included attempts by nationally known politicians to legislate against publishing anything with a strong sexual content that could be misconstrued as pornographic. At the same time, major corporations were busy buying up publications and laying off investigative writers whose job was to investigate them.

When I talked to Playboy they were angry with Gene so I sent proposals to Penthouse and Hustler Magazine. During this period, these men's magazines were publishing America's best literary authors and controversial subjects the mainstream media were afraid to touch. Both publications wanted the piece, but we ultimately went with Larry Flynt at Hustler Magazine. Gene's wrongful death lawsuit was settled out of court and he was awarded a seven-figure payout.

When I responded to Gene's email asking for help obtaining media attention for the young girl being held incommunicado by her family, he was surprised and taken aback that I was now working for the Scientologists. "Things are not what they appear, Gene," I assured him, and supplied him with the contact information of two aggressive and savvy digital media experts who might assist him.

Chapter Three

Rio Verde

A month or more later

Once in a while I run onto a subject so outrageous and troubling it's impossible not to be disgusted and filled with repugnance and outrage.

The period from 1950 to the late 1960s when the CIA and American Psychiatric community forced tens of thousands of innocent and vulnerable Americans into dangerous truth serum, mind control and brain washing experiments falls into this category. This period equals and in some cases exceeds the inhumanity of human testing conducted by the Nazis and its depravity and ruthlessness was without bottom.

Scientology founder L. Ron Hubbard was the first to discover these crimes and bring them to the public and he felt the sting of retribution because of it.

The unwitting victims – prisoners, soldiers, the hospitalized mentally ill and the average man on the street - were forced to endure overdoses of deadly and toxic drugs including LSD, psychoactive substances, hypnosis, convulsive electro-shock, sensory deprivation, prolonged isolation, psycho-surgery, deep sleep therapies, concussions, sexual abuse and every diabolical form of physical and psychological torture, including lobotomies. The result was catastrophic, criminal and deadly.

With the backing and support of U.S. intelligences services, psychiatrists implanted electronic transmitters into people's brains in an attempt to create robot assassins. When the results were unsatisfactory they simply disposed of the test subject/person by giving them a lobotomy and sending them to an asylum. They injected 37,000 military service men and prisoners with Metrazol, a convulsive agent that produces explosive seizures almost immediately after injection. It was hoped the substance would create a permanent state of amnesia, but instead it resulted in broken bones and teeth, permanent disability, mental illness and death.

While researching truth serums they subjected people to the drug Anectine that induces sensations of suffocation and drowning. The person experiences feelings of deep horror and terror as though he or she is on the brink of death. While in this condition they were interrogated, beaten, subjected to electro-shocks and scolded for misdeeds they had never done and told to reform or expect more of the same.

Psychiatrists working in Kentucky gave prison inmates extremely high does of LSD for 77 straight days. When they made the mistake of falling asleep they were attached to high voltage electroshock machines to wake them up. They dosed decorated armed forces personnel with massive doses of LSD without their knowledge. The result was a spate of suicides when these test subjects concluded they had gone insane. Many experienced lifelong anxiety, panic and nervous system disorders. They even tested high doses of LSD on colleagues and unsuspecting co-workers leading to the suicides and accidental deaths of renowned scientists.

According to a 1954 CIA memo, "No avenue of experimentation was ignored and no population was ruled out as being unfit to act as experimental guinea pigs. Men, women, children, prisoners, mental patients, criminal sexual psychopaths, schizophrenics, the elderly and even the terminally ill cancer patients were all used to perfect techniques of total control of the mind."

They even tested LSD on the unwitting public. They

spiked drinks at bars in New York City and San Francisco. They employed prostitutes to bring johns to safe houses equipped with cameras and listening devises and gave them LSD and other psychoactive substances. In 1960 they tested aerosol cans filled with deadly biological substances in a San Francisco neighborhood by releasing them into the air on a nearly hill. Eight people fell sick and died.

In 1947, as part of the Nuremberg War Crimes trail of Nazi leaders, the court established the Nuremberg Code. This code was used as a standard against which to judge German scientists who experimented with human subjects. It deeply impressed upon the world that experimentation on unknowing human subjects is morally and legally unacceptable.

In 1952, the CIA distributed a memo titled, Lobotomy and Related Operations." Part of this memo posed a question: "Is lobotomy a solution for disposal of an individual who might pose a security risk?" The document reported that a group of CIA scientists entertained the possibility of using the "icepick" lobotomy to render an individual harmless "from a security point of view."

At the time, Dr. Frank Freeman, a famous psychiatrist and the CIA's go-to man for lobotomy, described the operation as a surgically induced childhood. If the recipient of the operation did not die – and approximately 15 percent did – they were destined to sit quietly with their hands neatly folded in their laps or become bedridden in a persistent vegetative state. They would no longer be troublesome.

Freeman's most famous lobotomy patient was Rosemary Kennedy, the sister of President John F. Kennedy. At just 23 years old, Rosemary Kennedy was smart, beautiful and willful. She went under Freeman's ice pick procedure at her father, Joe's insistence. As a child, she had been eager to please, polite and responsible, but as she grew into her teenaged years, she became willful, wildly independent and violent, often throwing things at whoever displeased her. She was thought to have mild learning difficulties.

After Freeman's lobotomy, Rosemary was left with the mental capacity of a toddler – unable to walk, speak full sentences or follow simple directions. It took years for her to relearn basic skills like brushing her hair, bathing and dressing. She would never fully recover. She lived the majority of her life out of sight in institutions and died in a nursing home at the age of 74 in Massachusetts.

With unlimited and unwitting volunteers from mental institutions and prisons, Freeman streamlined his infamous transorbital ice-pick procedure. He started this procedure with three strong electric shocks to jolt patients into unconsciousness, and then using a hammer he drove an ice pick, many times from his own kitchen drawer, into the brain through the thin bone of the eye socket called the orbit. Then he swiveled and turned the pick back and forth making deep lacerations. Freeman was not trained or licensed as a surgeon, he deplored wearing gloves or a mask, and in later years, he performed lobotomies on desks at universities before large audiences.

Estimates of the total number of lobotomy procedures performed by the CIA and the larger psychiatric community range from 150,000 to 500,000 from 1950 to 1970. Of these at least 175,000 were total failures and people either died or had their lives ruined. As the failures added up, more and more hospitals refused to allow Dr. Freeman operating theaters for his procedure. In response, the once renowned psychiatrist took his show on the road. In the 1950s during a "lobotomy tour" to West Virginia and subsequently other states and driving his custom painted loboto-mobile he operated on 225 people in 12 days.

During an extended lobotomy tour, it is believed Freeman performed lobotomies on more than one thousand individuals and charged $25 a piece. He placed victims on counters or tables and without any kind of painkiller or anesthesia and many times before an audience he went to work. He descended into what some call a bizarre and brutal circus act whose example haunts the field of psychiatry today.

Breathtaking in its cruelty and sweeping in its insensitivity to humanity, leading American psychiatrists with tacit or full approval from the American Psychiatric Association and American Medical Association - bereft of any successful therapeutic treatment for mental illness - continued to subject innocent Americans to lobotomies for decades, while at the same time attacking Dianetics as a "mind healing" group and L. Ron Hubbard as being a quack.

In what is considered the most coldblooded and sadistic CIA and American psychiatrist endeavor was Psychic Driving developed by internationally prominent psychiatrist, Dr. Donald Ewan Cameron. In 1957 Cameron subjected mental patients to experiments that continue to shock and reverberate outrage generations later. With a CIA mandate to get results at all costs, psychic driving offers a looks at a depravity via unparalleled cruelty.

Cameron conducted brainwashing experiments on schizophrenic patients who were forced to lie naked under a searing red light for more than eight hours a day and for up to 8 months at a time. He placed these guinea pigs in electric wired heating cages until their temperature reached 102 degrees or more. He also pushed the limit on the over-utilized and worthless insulin coma therapy by putting subjects into coma for 24 hours a day for as many as 50 consecutive days.

Cameron's experiments, undertaken mostly on women, were designed to first "depattern" subjects by erasing their minds and memories and reducing them to the mental level of an infant or vegetable state, and then to "rebuild" their personality in a manner of his choosing. To achieve this, he first forced subjects through a regimen consisting of near fatal amounts of electroconvulsive shock therapy, drug-induced coma, sensory isolation and massive doses of LSD. In some cases, subjects were placed in drug or insulin comas for up to 88 days and received high voltage electric shocks – as many as 360 – for weeks or months while in coma. When fully depatterned, subjects were incontinent, unable to feed themselves and had no idea their name or location. In one case celebrated by the community, the first "depatterning" cycle turned a nineteen-year-old honors student into an infant who sucked her thumb, talked baby talk, demanded to be fed by bottle and urinated and defecated on the floor.

In a paper published in the American Journal of Psychiatry entitled "Psychic Driving" Cameron describes his brainwashing techniques. After depatterning was complete and the subject's mind was clean, he implemented stage two called "psychic driving." In this process he forced subjects to listen to repetitive messages such as "You are a good wife and mother and people love your company." These repeated messages were delivered through special helmets with speakers and designed so the user was in total darkness. The helmets were bound to their heads and they were strapped down in chairs. Subjects were forced to listened to messages for 20 hours a day up to weeks or months at a time. One subject strapped to a chair and blind-folded was forced to listen to the same message for 108 days straight.

In another experiment, a subject was forced into a destructive mind control experiment for one hundred days. This experimental "treatment" involved drug disinhibiting – a term used when near overdose amounts of drugs are forced on someone for a long period while keeping the subject asleep for weeks or months in psychological isolation. The treatment also included electro-convulsive-therapy at seventy-five percent higher dosage than the maximum level recommended by the American Psychiatric Association.

When complete, the subject had no memory of her

life previous to her treatments. She had been reduced to a vegetable and did not know her name, age, or where she was. She did not recognize her children and could not read or use a toilet. When told she had a husband, she did not know what a husband was.

These human guinea pigs were not told they were subjects in CIA and military mind control experiments and that the doctors attending to them were not acting in their best interest, but saw them as "human subjects" not relevant in the equation. Many psychiatrists involved viewed them as sub-human or as biological masses and were therefore unconcerned about their welfare or the outcomes in experiments.

During this period of national disgrace, the participation of psychiatrists, medical schools, hospitals, universities and private institutions was not a matter of a few scattered doctors or institutions pursuing questionable lines of investigation. Mind control experimentation was systematic and organized and involved leading psychiatrists and medical schools.

CHAPTER FOUR

SALT LAKE CITY

A CANCER GROW BOX

I love taking Trax, the new light rail system that stretches from city center to the far reaches of the Salt Lake valley and its bedroom communities. I jump on at Library Square just a block from my historic house downtown and can land just about anywhere in the valley. Today, I'm headed to Huntsman Cancer Center on the University of Utah Medical Center campus. The Sonoran Desert has my heart, but summers are so hot we relocate for a month or two to northern Utah where it's cool and we can enjoy my fabulous secret garden.

Today's visit to Huntsman will be the fifth in the last two months. Lana convinced me to take a day off and see a doctor after months of listening to my daily complaints. She sees that I'm tired and according to her, "You walk like an old man! You need to straighten up, you're always bent over."

My primary physician, an affable, if overworked man, ordered blood tests after examining me and noticed open sores on my forearm and another inside my ear.

"What's this?" he asked, pointing to my arm.

"Not really sure," I respond, "these sores and come and go. The big one here arrived a year or so ago."

A week later a dermatologist mapped 16 skin cancers on my torso and head. There were more in my ears and on my thighs and legs.

"You have what we call a skin cancer condition," he told me. "Patients with more than 12 active skin cancers are at a high risk for more serious problems."

Many biopsies later – and thankfully no melanoma – I undergo the first Mohs skin cancer tumor-removal surgery on my upper chest.

"Are you feeling any pain from the procedure?" the surgeon asks.

"No, I can't feel a thing. But I've been meaning to tell someone, I do have a good deal of pain in my breast." I pointed near my left nipple, "Right here."

"Yes, yes," he says, as his fingers quickly and expertly find the area. "There *is* something there – a mass. Does this hurt?" he presses down hard.

"Owh! Yes, that hurts!"

He steps back, stands straight up and looks ever so briefly into my eyes, then excuses himself. A few minutes later he returns with another doctor who introduces himself and examines my breast closely. "We need to take another biopsy," he says.

A few days later I get the news – breast cancer.

Lana's devastation is complete. We cry in one another's arms and try to let this new reality find a bottom. I comfort her, as has been my role with women for decades. Nothing prevails over this reality - not logic or pragmatics, not my existential foundation and not the Zen inspired *Be-Here-Now* breathing techniques I've often relied upon. Nothing. The ethos of belief - of individual belief – stitched together over a lifetime from eloquent personal reflections and metaphysical awe no longer work either. Powerful and beautiful ideas that have protected me turn to dust and the whirlwind scatters them to oblivion. For a time I am inert material, reduced to a pile of elemental lament, sadness, fear and disbelief. There is no bottom to this reality.

A week later, I take Trax to the University and Huntsman Cancer Center alone. The 6 a.m. riders are mostly young people wearing medical and support uniforms. On arrival we move into the main intake area together like an amorphous blob of humanity until we disburse and each person goes about his/her day. I walk to the surgery department alone where I am taken immediately into pre-op.

"Take off your clothes," a nurse tells me, "and put them into this plastic bag," she holds it up. "Put this gown on backside front." She shoots questions like bullets: "Did you eat or drink anything this morning? When was your last bowel movement? Are you on any medications? Are you allergic to any medications?"

An hour or two later, Dr. Andbacka, a tall and handsome Finlander, slices into my chest and removes a large cancerous tumor nestled in a bed of fatty tissue that is my left breast. When I awaken the tumor and many lymph nodes are gone – as is my left nipple and a good amount of my breast. In its absence is an eight-inch incision - closed with super glue – stretching from my sternum to my armpit.

Later in my room, my only visitor is my best friend Grant Bassett. We've been through much together.

Grant wants to know what it's like to be disfigured.

I corkscrew into my hospital bed and struggle to respond, "It's pretty much the same as being a fat fuck – only different," I finally respond. "You know all about that, right?"

We laugh until I cry and he hands me an ice cold Foster's Lager that he smuggled in. We drink beer, secretly vape THC and talk rubbish – hardly mentioning the operation. Before he leaves I hand him the empty can and tell him to return it to his trousers so he can impress the nurses on his way out. After he is gone I feel a deep emptiness and remorse – like I'm responsible for taking someone's life.

How could I have let this happen?

Monument Valley, Utah

A week after surgery, I pack my car and drive to Blanding, Utah where I spend the night. The next morning I head to the north end of Monument Valley. On a little-used dirt road, hidden from the highway by a hill, I park and hike off into the puzzle of ridges and valleys and flattop plateaus toward El Capitan, a famous monolith in the valley. From the roadway, El Capitan looks to be several hours away, but as I hike toward it, it seems to back off, moving farther away from me. The ground is carved by erosion and warped by pressure, taking me on side trips through intricate mazes of glens, grottoes, fissures, and passageways. I let my feet carry me, honoring the path as it presented itself, taking shapes and directions and detours I could not have predicted.

Stopping to eat some raisins and have a cool drink of water, I notice some mysterious shadowy canyons to the east. I decide not to capture their magic by exploring them. I have long resented science for its many revelations; when science solves a problem, the magic surrounding it evaporates. We unravel the secrets of the natural world too, reducing them to basic scientific principles and in doing so devalue them. We do the same thing to our spirit and soul. Instead of honoring the magic of our inner workings as it presents itself, we attempt to pick it apart as a scientist might, and something gets lost along the way.

I continue on, catching glimpses of El Capitan occasionally as I crest a hill or skirt around a bronze or vermillion-colored canyon system. It is much farther than I thought, and in the middle of the silence and burning rock I feel the weight of my health condition and surrender to the shadow of doubt and self-criticism that defeated me as a younger man. My nostrils are filled with the ripe, pungent perfume of sagebrush, while unnamed shades of umber, violet, and blue surround me as I make my way down into a canyon.

One footfall at a time, I go down into the labyrinth of my past defeats and remorse. The sun is on my face, yet shadows are all around me. Down I go into the place of dead ends, twisting canyons of excruciating pain and foolish self-centered narcissism. Down where the textures of the land are paradox: dried mud flats and countersunk potholes, overhangs and interlocking sediments, siltstone and stone sand dunes. The multiplicity of this nature – of my nature – demands I make this descent as part of my odyssey.

I slip by degrees into the lunacy that so characterizes modern man. I see the images of the two sons I sired but did not father. They stand defiantly before me on pillars of broken sandstone. The friends and lovers I retreated from are there too, crouching next to the alligator junipers. "I am guilty," I say out loud. I knew so little about life and even less about myself. I did not intend to hurt anyone, but everywhere I turned I created pain. I wish I'd been a better son and husband and father and lover. The ancient, ancient lies I told and the profoundly troubling mistakes of my youth waft down to me – one by one – from the hot wings of Hecate, the Goddess of Solitude.

The aboriginal Donne flutes call out to the boy in me. Descend into the ashes, they sing, before rising into the light of manhood. But it is more difficult in my culture, I answer. The descent takes much longer. I am the only person who can grant me forgiveness, and I have learned I must refuse. Like the Greek god Prometheus, lashed to a rock and destined to have his liver ripped from his abdomen every new day, I must stand tall, bare my chest, and wait with arms outstretched. I promise to always remember the hurt and pain I have caused. I am truly sorry.

I walk on through the tears until I can see as a child sees, and the wonder and magic of my own mysterious life returns. I understand the voices of lunacy and the need to face my demons. For me, peace lies along the simple dirt path before me. From it, I can view my life stretching out before me and behind me. The path affords me a fresh vision and the necessary idealism to face the world at large. My modern culture wants me to sidestep negative moods and emotions, yet the simple path into wilderness forces me to observe what is really within my heart and soul. Nature befriends my problems, it allows for my mistakes, and it offers me the latitude to be human.

It is not enough to seek only the light. To find true peace, I must visit the land of shadow and defeat. I must walk along the hot and dusty path to the place where my shadow resides. The true spirit of transcendence and the lofty quest for the highest vision are found along this trail.

Picking my way out of the canyon, I spot El Capitan on the southern horizon. I am no closer to it than when

I began. From some high turrets I watch the heat shimmering off the burning hogback ridges between me and the obelisk. This place possesses the special beauty of all wild and lonely things. At the horizon, spread out across its length, sail-like clouds touch the alabaster towers of the valley. I remember what Everett Ruess wrote to a friend about Monument Valley:

It has all been a beautiful dream, sometimes tranquil, sometimes fantastic, and with enough pain and tragedy to make the delights possible by contrast. But the pain too has been unreal. The whole dream has been filled with warm and cool but perfect colors and aesthetic contemplations... Alone on the open desert I have made up songs of wild, poignant rejoicing and transcendent melancholy.

I will not make it to El Capitan on this day. Perhaps I will never make it that far. After a long rest, I turn back and do not make it to my car until deep dusk.

Chapter Five

Rio Verde

A few days later

Lana is in the kitchen trying out a new recipe. She loves to cook and moves like a dancer whose every gesture is choreographed by a movement vocabulary that speaks of art, intellect and the joy of discovery. Yet tonight she is betraying her natural stylish performance. A misstep here and a shaky hand there.

Lana is one of the most beautiful and elegant people I have ever met.

"A glass of Cab?" I ask, inspecting a bottle in the panty.

"Yes, please," she says cutting vegetables and keeping her back to me.

"I'll have one with you."

I'm an interloper in her kitchen, standing here or there and always in the way.

"Any progress today?" she asks.

"It's hard," I respond, opening the bottle and taking a deep breath. "Too much to think about, to take in... to consider."

The chopping stops and she grips the counter with both hands.

I place the glass of wine next to her and tenderly kiss her neck and ear. "You okay, baby?"

She starts to say something, but stops and holds the counter as if falling. She shakes her head back and forth and then drops it forward.

"It's alright, baby," I say in my manly voice. "We will see this through."

Suddenly, she turns and rushes forward, throwing her arms around my neck and buries her head into my chest. She sobs uncontrollably. "I'm sorry... I'm sorry... I'm just so scared!"

We embrace as if it might be for the last time and we both just cry.

Pulling back she looks at me as if she had never seen me before, "I want you to know that no matter what happens I'll be there and always love you and take care of you..."

Now, Ava, Lilmum, Aimee and Pierre, our pups, are in the kitchen, too. They surround us and throw themselves against our legs. Ava arcs her head up and howls a mournful howl. They want the Big Dad to know they are there to help, too. We are a famdamnly.

Holding my arms with her hands and looking up deeply into my eyes, she sobs, "I don't know what to do! I wish none of this ever happened...

"I know baby. I know... Me too..." I say through my own tears, "I'm so sorry you have to be part of this... I wish I could do something to make it all go away... To save you from this..."

We embrace and hold each other tightly. The dogs are swinging their rear-ends into us now and nearly knocking us over. We start laughing through the tears and offer hugs and loves to each of our tender children.

Little does either of us know that this is just the beginning of a journey from which I am destined to never return.

In the morning, we drive into Fountain Hills for breakfast at Lana's favorite greasy spoon. The ten-mile drive wends its way between the Yavapai-Apache Nation Indian reservation and the McDowell Nature preserve. The washed-out desert hills are populated by hundreds of drought-stricken but proud saguaro cactus trees, dead-looking creosote bushes and broken-down crown-of-thorns cacti. Lana listens to old time rock-and-roll and gifts me with world-class smiles. She is happy to be on the road with her man.

At Phil's our booth is open so we plop down in the red leather tuck-and-roll seats. Phil's Café is a successful rec-reation of a thousand-and-one lost to time eateries where as kids we sat in the booths and shared giant plates of real French fries and catsup. The walls are covered in original Coca-a-cola posters, ephemera and advertising art. It has that sweet feeling of comfort that speaks of temporary ownership like the *real* hangouts of our past. There's some-thing else about Phil's - everything is a bit run-down and undone – just the way it was long ago. On the floor next to the men's room is an old coffee canister filled with bacon grease that someone stores there before taking it out.

Lana abruptly sits straight up in her seat and starts singing along with the piped in music. It's Del Shannon's, Little Town Flirt. "Here she comes with that look in her eye," she belts out and smiles with eyes dancing. "Oh, she's lookin' at you and you know she's going to treat you wrong so your heart just better be strong because you can get hurt messin' around with that little town flirt…"

I adore the little girl in Lana. In the big city she is a

sophisticated executive, making impressive deals in corporate America, but then she cuts loose and transforms into a little girl who just wants to laugh and have fun.

I order buttermilk pancakes and eggs and Lana gets the California omelet with avocado, fresh tomatoes and potatoes. She is happy about the plate of good food in front of her, and it is easy to see the simplicity of her soul all wrapped up in a complex contemporary life.

If Lana and I were a love story written for the stage, we would be a three-act play with the second act missing.

It was a brisk autumn night in 1965 at the Cinnamon Cinder teen club in Salt Lake City when Lana and I set eyes on one another for the first time. She was fourteen and I was sixteen. I spotted her across the foyer and moved quickly to ask her to dance. After that first song, instead of turning and going our separate ways we just stand there happily talking - as if we had known one another for a lifetime. She was a ninth grader at Hillcrest Junior High and I was starting my junior year at Murray High. She was tall, willowy, blonde and beautiful. Her smile took my breath away and I was smitten.

When the band played a slow song and I wrapped my arms around her our bodies were a perfect fit – as if made for one another. I held her tight but she pulled back just enough to give me a coquettish smile, then pulled me even closer. In that moment something magical happened and we both knew it. We spent the entire night on the dance floor hoping it would never end. After the band's last song we reluctantly parted and I asked if she might be there next Friday. She smiled and said she'd be there. Back with my friends, Randall and Clark wanted to know everything about this mysterious blonde and if she might have girl-friends.

As the club emptied I spotted Lana and friends wait-ing for a ride. A friend dropped them off and promised to be back but hadn't shown up. 'If you need a ride,' I said, 'we'd be happy to help.' They happily accepted and Lana sat next to me in the front seat and leaned in close against me. At her house I walked her to the door and asked if I could call her. Flashing that stunning smile she gave me her number.

Within weeks we were inseparable. We were an item at school and walked the halls arms and legs intertwined akimbo. From that first night at the dance club until a few weeks before I graduated nearly two years later Lana and I were the quintessential high school sweethearts. On a cold winter's night in 1966 the film *Camelot* premiered and we clung to one another and cried in disbelief at the love story turned into a betrayal playing out before us. We promised no complicated love triangle would ever come between us.

Even as Lana and I found love everywhere, an exciting and sometimes troubling new day was breaking out in America. Images of racism in the south flashed across our television screen, as did American boys fighting and dying in Vietnam half the world away. We found joy and solace in the music of the day, but battles over long hair, changing fashions and opposing viewpoints created family and societal turmoil, threatening to tear us all apart. The children of the greatest generation wanted change and we wanted it now.

As this cultural war took root we spent our nights finding adventure and sublime pleasure in each other's arms. We were desperate lovers, demanding nothing more than being together. In so many ways, America was simpler then and we shared a sweet tenderness and hopeful naiveté that youth gifted us.

After breakfast we drive to Scottsdale and the famous Barrett and Jackson Auto show. While I care little about cars Lana and her family are car crazies. Her brother Ron built a warehouse just to house his dozen Corvettes and rare sports vehicles. After reading a lifetime's worth of literature and philosophy, I viewed automobiles – and most modern conveniences - as a proletariat might: an automobile is a machine with four wheels and a coach designed to safely get me from Point A to Point B. But when Lana catches sight of a Ferrari or McLaren she sees escape, adventure, romance, sex and a big house with extra garage space to park her BMW and dream machines.

Notwithstanding my disinterest, I am a history buff and The Barrett and Jackson brings the rarest, most iconic and historic cars together. As Lana wanders the huge showrooms searching for the perfect dream machine I sit on the sideline and drink a pint or two irreverently criticizing the parade of wanna-be big-daddy-Warbucks and beautiful women.

Lana's parents divorced and her father, Larry, owned a popular nightclub, The Blackhawk Club, and was a man about town. He was strict and kept a close eye on Lana. In a painful default she became the woman of the house at age twelve. She kept house, cooked, did the laundry and watched over her two younger brothers, Ron and Storm. I had no idea of the deep heartache she carried because of the divorce and the suffering she went through. Just as today, Lana keeps pain to herself.

Away from Lana, I had a separate life with my friends, spending much of my time listening to or playing music, driving around endlessly with anyone who had a license or hanging out with my best friend, Randall Potts. For years my plan after graduation was to escape my little town and never look back. I was determined to strike out and live life as I saw fit, and to repudiate the values of American materialism and consumerism. The siren song of youth fueled my desire to live outside on the edge and to explore all I knew so little about.

Late one night in March of 1967 after Lana and I made love her father discovered a condom wrapper lying on the floor next to her bed. He was furious and called my house and spoke to my mother. He demanded I come to the house for a talk. I remember driving over and preparing to fight it out if I had to. Lana sat on a recliner and I was on the living room couch. Instead of raising his voice in anger, Larry asked if I loved Lana and said if I truly did, the last thing I would want for her is to get her pregnant and ruin her life. He appealed to the budding man inside me and encouraged me to man up and do the right thing. I was surprised at his arguments and accepted what he said. I agreed to stop seeing Lana.

Of course it didn't turn out that way. We continued

our relationship and added another layer of precautions, lies and deceit. There was a sense of fear as if every moment together might be our last. After the meeting with her father, I couldn't shake the feeling of guilt. Because I had already planned leaving town I decided it best to say goodbye to my lover.

On our last Friday night date I took Lana to our favorite Italian Restaurant, the Cinegrill, and over lasagna and spaghetti I told her I was breaking off our relationship and felt we should not see each other again. I will never forget the hurt and pain in her face. She looked me, then slowly turned away and lowered her head so I could not see her face and cried.

The morning after graduation Randall took me to the airport and I purchased a one-way ticket to San Francisco. Unknowingly, it turned out to be the famous Summer of Love and I was swept up in the Haight Ashbury cloud of marijuana smoke, LSD trips and tens of thousands of people like me. I never stopped loving Lana but I was now on my way to discover the big outside world and the real authentic me.

A few years later, I learned Lana married and moved to Australia with her husband and two small sons. For the next forty-seven years I had no idea where she was or what she was doing. I always hoped I'd run into her and I regretted breaking her heart and leaving. I never stopped wondering about Lana and her life. On the acknowledgement page to my books, I always list the people I love and those who held a special place in my heart. Lana's name was always listed. In one of my novels, Chaco: A Tale of Ancient Lives, I named one of the main characters after her.

In May of 2014 while reading the online version of the Salt Lake Tribune I happened on an obituary for Storm Mitchell. There was no doubt it was Lana's baby brother. I remember him as a boy of six or seven. He was precocious and wore a Beatle haircut. In rapid fire, he'd ask one question after another and always had a big wide toothy smile. The picture of the man who died was nothing like the boy I remembered. As I read the obituary my heart fluttered when I saw Lana's name. It read, sister Lana Hicks, Kansas City, Missouri. It was the first substantiated bit of evidence I had of her in all those years.

The online obituary tribute offered an option to respond with condolences. I wrote a simple acknowledgment and ended it with an invitation to anyone in her family to get together and reminisce about those long-ago days. Two weeks later, at a point I thought a response was unlikely, I received an email from her. Like me, she had wondered what happened to me and wanted to meet as soon as possible.

Lana and I lost our Second Act. We've been together for four years now.

Chapter Six

Rio Verde

A week later

Going through the reams of high value, confidential and upper echelon material sent me by Scientology leadership, I realized that after years of arms-length mistrust of me as a non-member, I am now free to explore the inner workings of the church.

When in LA my office is at SMC (Scientology Media Center) located at the onetime Majestic Studios on Sunset Boulevard in Hollywood. The famous five-acre historic film studio dates to the Golden Age of Hollywood films and opened in 1911. Its sound stages and recording studios produced *The Birth of the Nation, El Cid, Invasion of the Body Snatchers* and a hundred others. Scenes from *The Wizard of Oz* were shot there, too. The church purchased the studio and remodeled it with state-of-the-art broadcasting studios, computer and robotically controlled cameras and visual effects center.

My involvement with the Scientologists stretches back to 2010 when Ben Shaw, the Director of the Office of External Affairs, contacted me and requested I come to Clearwater, Florida. He was impressed by my investigative pieces on Kip Eliason and my investigative expose of the American evangelist Jimmy Swaggart, commissioned by Larry Flynt of Hustler Magazine. I was in the pews when the fleshy-faced Swaggart tearfully blubbered out his now infamous sound bite, "I have sinned!" I went undercover and assumed a new identity to expose Swaggart's kinky sex addictions and his bilking of hundreds of millions of dollars from naïve cable audiences worldwide.

My first trip to Clearwater was a whirlwind of activities: meetings with high ranking executives, public relations operatives during the day and evenings at the study center facilities where hundreds of ardent scientologists rushed from one place to another on a mission to advance his or her spiritual journey to reach *Clear*. I endured long days zoning-out to church indoctrination videos and taking a guided tour of the gulf coast city where the church bought up the mostly rundown historic section of town – more than 150 buildings – and transformed it into the church's world ecclesiastical epicenter. At night I dined at one of Fort Harrison's four restaurantsn then retired to a suite on the upper floor of the first class hotel.

On subsequent trips to Clearwater I lived at Fort Harrison, the opulent nineteenth century rococo-style hotel that serves VIPs and is the church's spiritual flagship. Members refer to it as Flag. In the mornings from my window I watch the street below as bus after bus disgorges thousands of Sea Org (Sea Organization) members who work in its downtown headquarters. Each sign a billion year contract and take their commitment to the church and its work seriously. They arrive from church-owned apartment complexes in the suburbs and are identically attired in nondescript black slacks and shoes and white shirts. Men wear ties and the women eschew make-up and jewelry. Each carries books or folders or brief cases and has a blackberry pager attached to his or her belt. They move with a sense of deliberation, seldom smiling or showing animation as they make their way to appointed workplaces.

The most attractive Sea Org members work in highly visible positions – such as at Flag – where they come into contact with well-heeled members and non-members. Many are bilingual and come from east European and South American countries, lured here for religious enlightenment and an American green card work visa.

I got the impression that Shaw was searching for someone willing to go undercover to infiltrate and investigate individuals or target groups. To my pleasant surprise he gives me carte blanche to write about anything I found interesting. He offered great pay, an expense account, unlimited travel, and I set my own deadlines. These kinds of contract assignments exist only in dreams. According to Shaw, they were in the process of starting a Florida edition of Freedom Magazine, the chruch's investigative periodical published in Hollywood, California. The California edition went off the rails a year or two earlier because of disagreements between the power centers of LA and Clearwater and was currently taking a hiatus. Shaw wanted to get as many first-rate writers on board to generate articles in advance of the Florida edition premiere.

Two months later I receive a call from Shaw on Sunday morning asking if I'd seen the cover story that day in the St. Petersburg Times attacking the church. I hadn't, of course, but he wanted me to catch an afternoon flight to Clearwater to discuss an important hush-hush assignment. He mentioned Tommy Davis, the brash Hollywood-based lightning rod church spokesperson, who wanted to meet me before returning to California.

The article in question, Scientology Benefits when

Miami Dentist Runs Up Patients Bills, was the cover story in the Sunday edition. It was part of the steady diet of St. Petersburg Times stories attacking the church. The story revolved around a dentist accused of employing unethical practices to trick patients into signing up for treatment plans that included large fees for extensive dental work and arranging financing with major credit card companies which he was paid for in advance. After obtaining the patient's money he failed to perform the procedures.

The dentist, Dr. Rene Piedra, was the most successful and showy dentist in the state and was a well-known Scientologist. The paper alleged Piedra employed Scientology business philosophies that transformed his practice into a moneymaking machine for the benefit of his church. It blamed Piedra's scam squarely on the shoulders of L. Ron Hubbard and used Hubbard's quotes from generations old policy papers to back up its claims. Piedra went from making a hundred thousand dollars in 2000 to raking in more than $4.7 million just three years later. Over a six-year period, Piedra made ten million and donated seven-hundred-thousand to church building and services projects.

Not surprisingly, the church was furious. It maintained it had nothing to do with Piedra's practice and his contributions were given freely to support the church's aggressive building projects.

The story of today's Church of Scientology cannot be told without telling the companion story of the overarching animus, hostility and even hatred between it and members of the media. This animosity started in the early 1970s when the church arrived on the Sun Coast of Clearwater, Florida and ran headlong into the buzz saw of one of the most influential and powerful newspapers in America, the St. Petersburg Times, now renamed The Tampa Bay News.

Much of what the public knows about the church comes from the pages of the Tampa Bay News. Today, over forty years and 7000 negative stories and a multitude of lawsuits later, the Tampa Bay News and the Church of Scientology are locked in an intractable battle. On one side is the fastest growing, richest, and most outspoken new church in American history, and on the other side, an old-guard media giant with a reputation of being one of the toughest and best newspapers in American history.

An inside informant and past Tampa Bay News editor characterizes the battle to me this way, "It's an epic and titanic struggle between two powerful groups who have no way to disengage. It's a protracted struggle at the leadership level now, and its origins are lost in hatred."

On arrival in Clearwater, I was whisked away to a

private conference room at Flag where Shaw and his boss, Peter Mansell wanted to negotiate an investigation of St. Petersburg Times and its Publisher, Paul Tash, and Editor-in-Chief, Joe Childs. Together, these two were the most powerful newspapermen in Florida.

"What would you like me to find out about Tash and Childs?" I asked.

"Everything!" Shaw answered.

"Tash and Childs are looking for a Pulitzer at our expense. They've been publishing a steady stream of lies, half-truths and falsehoods about us for years." Mansell added. "They will go any length…"

"Tash is the chairman of the Pulitzer (Prize) board," Shaw interrupts, "and Childs is dying to get the prize before he retires."

"How would you like me to proceed?"

Both men push back in their plush, oversized high-back leather chairs and exhale. "That's up to you, Mark," Ben smiles. "You are the expert."

"Do what you do," Peter adds. "We want dirt. We want you to go through their lives from start to this moment. We want to find out who they are and what they do when they aren't playing news king- pins."

"Undercover?" I ask.

"You don't need to tell us, Mark. We want results, not a thesis on means."

I told them about the Swaggart investigation and how I spent three months undercover infiltrating the organization, volunteering my time to the congregation, making friends, attending meetings, joining the single's group, donating money and identifying business practices such as employing relatives and researching sweetheart deals that seemed too good to be true or right. After three months, I surfaced and conducted a traditional investigation scouring court records, interviewing enemies, making connections in the legal and law enforcement worlds and talking to hateful ex-employees and business associates.

"Does this sound like a workable plan?"

Neither answered directly, but Shaw said, "We will leave that up to you."

Mansell added, "We want you to talk to their sixth grade teacher, their hometown school friends, college, and especially their ex-girlfriends…"

"We know Tash had an affair," Shaw adds, "and was involved in an ugly divorce. See if his ex-wife will talk. There are a lot of disgruntled ex-employees who might talk, too."

"You don't need to tell us how you are going to operate. We want results."

It was obvious they did not want to know the details for reasons of plausible deniability. They wanted results by any means necessary.

"Okay, I think I get it," I started. "Of course, we are talking about a long-term investigation, right? It could take six months, a year or even more. We can go down this road and find all the material you'll ever want or we could end up with a big fat nothing. Zip."

Neither seemed phased by the timeline but incredulous at the idea there might be nothing out there on these two targets.

The idea of this investigation, its size, scope and complexity pleased me. I could parachute into places across the country and around the world on the Scientologists' dime and do the type of investigation few of my ilk ever dreamed of. I was in and told them so.

"There's only one thing left to discuss," I said sitting back and stretching my hands and arms up and over my head, "compensation."

"We've been thinking about that," Shaw says. "Would you consider an open-ended contract at ten thousand a month and all expenses?"

I paused to consider the offer. It was 2010, the middle of the great recession and tens of thousands of journalists were being laid off and major newspapers were folding every day. Moreover, the publishing world was stuck between the recession and the transition from print to the electronic delivery of content.

"I pay my own taxes?"

Both smirked.

"Yes, Mark," Mansell answered, "You will be required to file your own tax returns. You will not be on our payroll. This is a work-for-hire contract, not an offer of employment. You are your own boss."

"Okay then, let's get to work."

Suffice it to say, investigating the publisher and editor of one of the most influential papers in America was going to be a difficult and arduous feat.

The next morning, I try breakfast at the patio restaurant in Flag's courtyard. It is a beautiful setting with exotic flowering plants, palm trees and a tropical bird in a giant ostentatious cage. The enclosure includes a swimming pool, cabana bar and high stucco walls offering the feeling of luxury, security and seclusion. My server, Mia, is young, beautiful and friendly.

"I've seen you before, right?" she asks.

"I've been here for a few days."

"Taking advanced training?"

"No, I work with Ben Shaw. I'm not a member of the church."

Her surprise is obvious. She darts a look around, scanning the area quickly, "What do you do?"

"I'm a writer."

"Oh, I've always wanted to be a writer," she says smiling. "What do you write about?"

"I've pretty much done it all, but this time around I'm working as an investigative writer," I notice she is looking at my iPhone on the table.

"Here, take a look." I hand it to her. I just bought my first iPhone and few people have seen one up close.

"I… I don't want a cell phone," she replied nervously.

"You don't? I thought everyone wanted one."

"I don't even know what they do," she pauses, "Well, I'd like one, but no one here even has a cell."

"Take a look," I say again and hand the handset to her. She rubs her thumbs across its slick and smooth face.

"Are they off limits?"

"No, I don't know."

"You Sea Org?"

She hands the device back and excuses herself. She has other customers. A few minutes later she returns.

"Yes, I'm Sea Organization."

"Clear?"

She smiles, embarrassed, "Working on it."

She's still admiring the iPhone so I hand it back to her.

"We don't get paid really, so no one can afford a cell phone."

"Would you like one if you could?"

"Not really," she says in a detached tone. "We have lots to do and cell phones are such a distraction."

I hold my hand out and she reluctantly returns the phone.

"May I ask you a question?"

"Sure," she winces, noticeably.

"How did you become a Sea Org member?"

She smiles and proudly answers, "My family are members and I always wanted to be one."

"You were raised in the church?"

"Yes, five of us."

Nodding at a waiter nearby, I ask, "Do all of the people who work at Flag have family in the church?"

"Oh, no. Just a few of us."

Later I head down Harrison Street to Starbucks and watch Sea Org members spill out of church owned buildings onto the busy sidewalks while I do online research and plan my investigation. The single-minded dedication these individuals bring to the church is laudable and spooky. Few have the time or resources for the church owned Starbucks. They receive room and board from the church and a few dollars a month for expenses.

From there, I head south thirty-five miles to St. Petersburg to scope out the offices of the St. Petersburg Times. In a brash and stupid moment, I park and head inside the foyer where I ask to speak with Editor-in-Chief Joe Childs. The receptionist asks if I have an appointment and tells me he is not available. Next I find the high-end neighborhoods where Tash and Childs live. At Childs' residence I park up the street and walk along the sidewalk to a place I can look into the backyard. One confidential document given to me said he was known for growing marijuana and I wanted to see if it was true.

Back in St. Petersburg, I stop at the Side Street bar, a favorite after work watering hole where alcohol-addled journalists bend their elbows in an age-old scribe ritual. The place is empty so I head back over to the Times' employee parking and hunker down, hoping to catch Childs or Tash when they leave.

It is important to maintain my anonymity and work behind the scenes for as long as possible. I need to get up-to-speed, collect essential information and evidence and establish a strong foundation for building a solid and un-assailable story. I have to figure out how to gain access to insider information or somehow infiltrate the Times organization. The paper is not hiring so that is out, and in fact, it's laying journalists off and shrinking its operation. Until I find a solution, I'll keep up the surveillance and see what I can dredge up.

The next few days are spent reading confidential documents outlining the results of private investigations funded by the church on scores of St. Petersburg Times reporters, editors, advertisers and supporters. The sheer volume of information collected by the church amazes me and take up a terabyte of computer storage.

It soon becomes evident that I need to change my location. It is fair to assume that the church's many enemies in the greater Tampa Bay area might be watching the comings and goings at the Fort Harrison Hotel and my covert inquiry could be in jeopardy. It is in everyone's best interest that I find other accommodations.

After making reservations at another hotel for the next day, I receive a call from Ben Shaw. He wants me to meet Mary Repper for breakfast in the morning. Repper is a well-connected political operative in the bay area and on contract with the church to offer views, opinions and advice. I voice my concern about maintaining my anonymity but Shaw seems unconcerned. He says Repper could help me and she and Tom Cruise were best friends and he might come along with her.

The next morning I'm up early, dress leisurely for a business breakfast and meeting and take the elevator from the ninth floor to the lobby where Ben is waiting. When the door opens I'm confronted by hundreds of smartly dressed men and women crowding the lobby. Ben is standing front and center waving me forward. My first instinct is to escape, to hit the close door button and disappear back to my room. Instead, I confidently move forward where Ben stands with two distinguished looking men wearing dark suits. My first thought - lawyers.

"Mark Taylor," Ben says smiling and in a formal voice, "I want you to meet the honorable Dick Greco, Mayor of Tampa Bay."

I reach out, take his hand and shake it, "Very happy to meet you, Mr. Mayor," I look to Ben and raise my eyebrows.

"And this is Everett Rice," Ben goes on, "Pinellas County Chief of Police."

Oh my God! I think to myself. After shaking his hand, I turn to Ben and in a good-natured way ask, "Ben, what's happening here? Is this a convention or something?"

"Didn't anyone tell you? It's our annual community breakfast. Once a year we invite friends from all over to come for an open house breakfast."

Turning to the men, Ben adds, "Mark is a nationally known investigative journalist. He's the guy who brought down Jimmy Swaggart in Louisiana. He's working with us now on stories about the St. Petersburg Times."

My knees buckle. I'm happy to get such a kind introduction but feel steamrolled and betrayed. The two dignitaries laugh about Swaggart and follow up with disparaging comments about the St. Pete Times and the unfair coverage each received from them. They wish me success in getting some dirt on the newspaper. Rice hands me his business card and tells me to call him. "I might have a lead for you."

Ben excuses us, "There are some other people waiting to meet Mark. Thanks so much for joining us this morning."

The foyer is filled to capacity and Ben leads me up the grand staircase to the mezzanine ballroom where more than a thousand people are already eating, visiting or milling around. It is a festive gathering.

"Ben," I exclaim taking his arm and stopping him,

"there goes my undercover identity!"

"Oh," he replies, "I'm sorry Mark, but we want people to know what you are doing."

I am dumbfounded and pissed. We agreed I would work undercover in an attempt to infiltrate the Times and here Ben is introducing me to the Who's Who of Tampa Bay. By the time we work our way to our table he had introduced me to CEOs of large companies, influential law firm attorneys and the director of the church's volunteer ministry. At our table, I meet Mary Repper.

"Oh Mark, I'm so glad to finally meet you," she says, offering her hand, "Ben has shared some of your work with me and I'm impressed. So happy to see you are onboard."

"Very pleased to meet you too, Mary. It's great to be in good company. I've heard good things about you as well."

I am furious but play along, trying to figure out why Shaw is openly flaunting my presence and background. Later, I learn that the war between the church and St. Pete Times is open and celebrated among central Floridians. I was a top gun hired to root out dirt on the enemy.

Over the next months I learn if you are an important political figure or high-profile individual in the Tampa Bay area and you aren't being attacked or sued by an enemy or competitor something is wrong. Conversely, if you aren't attacking or suing someone something is wrong. There is a lot of money here and most high rollers have lawyers and private detectives on the payroll. It is a sordid cesspool of sharks and alligators - and I have just been dropped into the middle of it. Not unlike Louisiana, central Florida has a banana republic persona, complete with histories, rules and war games.

The breakfast was therefore filled with like-minded individuals who had been skewered and roasted by the powerful and vindictive St. Pete Times.

"Tom's not joining us?" Ben asks Repper.

"He should be, he was coming with Tommy Davis," she responds. "They should have been here an hour ago."

Mary gives Ben a look of discomfort.

"Mary is the best chef on the west coast," Ben boasts. "Tom will sometimes come to town without telling anyone just to have Mary bake him one of her famous coconut pies."

Mary blushes and tells everyone how Tom arrived this week in a rented red corvette and stayed at her house for the weekend just to get away and have a coconut pie to himself.

At my first opportunity, I excuse myself saying I am going to try the buffet, but quickly make my way to the exit where I run into Peter Mansell, Ben's partner and boss.

"Peter, I want you to know how upset and angered I am about you blowing my cover!"

Peter squares himself as I tell him the damage they have done to my investigation. He listens intently and apologizes. As he finishes, he points to a group of well-dressed African American men a short distance away. Taking me by the sleeve of my sports coat he leads me to them.

"Reverend Shabazz," Mansell says to one of them. "Thank you so much for coming. It is wonderful to see you."

Shabazz is the leader of the Nation of Islam in Florida and a right-hand man to Louis Farrakhan.

"Peter," Shabazz responds, "good to see you. Thank you for the invitation. You have quite a turn out today. Congratulations."

Three men wearing black suits, pencil thin ties and dark glasses surround Shabazz.

"Thank you reverend, I'd like to talk to you privately before you leave, but for now I want to introduce you to Mark Taylor. He is an investigative journalist working for us."

We shake hands and nod, "It's an honor," I say and he bows graciously.

Along with dignitaries, I am introduced to many ranking members of the church including Ben's wife, Maria, who is the corporate president of the Church of Scientology.

Back at the table, Repper dials up numbers trying to locate Tom Cruise and Tommy Davis. They are the breakfast's main attraction and everyone is waiting for them to arrive.

I see Ben and he is waving me over. He is with two handsome older Sicilian men. I learn later they are part of the New York, Miami and Italian mafia. They arrived in the Miami area in the early 1960s and developed hotels and golf course resorts. They wear expensive sharkskin suits and look as if they just walked out of Sardi's in New York from some earlier era. They are the Vincent brothers and well known in south Florida. While telling us a story about the early days in Miami, Tony raises his arm gesticulating and I notice a flashy watch on his wrist. When he sees me admiring it, he slips it off his wrist and hands it to me.

"You like this watch?" he asks, smiling.

"It's very nice," I answer.

"It's yours," he says and smiles.

The watch is a Rolex with diamonds set around the clock face. Before I could say anything else, Ben takes the watch from my hand and returns it, saying, "Tony, Mark can't accept gifts. He is working for us."

The man looks at Ben, then at me, nodding and smiling, "I hope one day you might write something for us."

Smiling from ear to ear, I answer, "It would be my pleasure."

CHAPTER SEVEN

THE HOLE IN THE ROCK TRAIL –
GARFIELD COUNTY, UTAH
DATE: AUGUST 2019

Diving into the desert wilderness, I power down the rugged Hole in the Rock trail, following Everett Ruess' path to the last place he was known to have been seen. The dirt road welcomes me. There are few signs of man out here, only the dusty dirt road that circles the landscape like a cowboy's lasso. In the sky above, an occasional airline glints in the sun and look like a perfect silver crucifix pointing west.

Whatever happened out here on this landscape millions of years ago was cataclysmic. Cauldrons of red-hot pig iron poured over the land; oceans flooded, flourished, and receded, great land masses buckled up and became cannon fodder for volcanic artillery pieces, and now it all lies in repose, strewn haphazardly across the landscape. An easy peace mantles the corpses of this Armageddon today. The rain and wind have softened its edges, and time has brought the beauty of decay.

Everett visited red-rock country for the first time in 1931 and immediately knew he belonged here. Until he disappeared, he ranged over the sagebrush and cedar forests, climbed the towering ridges, and explored the deep winding canyons. While fascism blossomed in Europe and the grapes of wrath ripened in the American dust bowl, the young Everett Ruess beat a solitary path into the heart of this expansive wilderness.

In late autumn 1934, with only his burros as companions, Everett traveled down the old Mormon Hole in the Rock trail on his way to the Grand Canyon. His plan was to winter in the hidden canyons of the Escalante Drainage and Glen Canyon. Few had visited these narrow winding canyons since the ancient Ancestral Puebloans lived in them hundreds of years earlier.

By mid-afternoon, I arrive at the deserted camp where ten days after he departed Escalante, Everett camped with two sheepherders. Five months later, in the wet spring of 1935, the sheepherders told searchers that he left their camp on the morning of November 17, heading east in the direction of Davis Gulch. It is the last time he is known to have been seen.

This land does not give up its secrets willingly; it exacts a price from those who seek to discover the source of its allure and power. Today, this land signifies more the contemporary view of transcendence than perhaps any other place on earth. Everett was not the first to be drawn here, nor will he be the last. Men have searched this outback for pieces of their soul. They arrived restless and leave changed.

No one knows how long Everett stayed in Davis Gulch before he disappeared – leaving behind little more than his footprints in the deep sand to be found the next spring. Even though Everett's vanishing act began earlier, it was accomplished here. Remarkably, the last real word from him still makes the journey back to us today. Through his letters, poems, and essays – composed for family and friends and published widely after his disappearance – he beckons us forward; inviting us to join him on the pathway across the land he loved so intensely.

The view from the sheepherder's camp is spectacular. To the west, less than a half mile away, the cliffs of Fifty Mile Ridge dominate the horizon and appear more like some exaggerated Hollywood backdrop than a world-class upthrust of Kayenta sandstone. To the north, east, and southeast, the land is an endless jumble of deep winding gorges and canyons that cut through a seventy-five-square-mile tract of broken rock and petrified sand dunes. To the south, twenty miles away, Navajo Mountain climbs nearly 10,000 feet and sets an anchor in the sky. The Navajo Gods live there.

Six months before his disappearance, Everett camped on Navajo Mountain. In a letter to a friend, he wrote about the place where he eventually disappeared: *"The country to the north is as rough and impenetrable a territory as I have ever seen. Thousands of domes and towers of sandstone lift their rounded pink tops from blue and purple shadows."*

I explore the campsite in the blistering heat, sensing his presence. "I know what happened to you," I say aloud. I am convinced the original search conducted in March of 1935 and the subsequent searches that summer were not only flawed, but also totally inadequate. For a decade I conducted my own painstakingly slow, but thorough search of the area. I made discoveries and tracked down leads no one expected to find. And I developed my own theory about Everett's disappearance, and like all good investigators, I set out to disprove myself.

Over the years, theories have been put forth, searches have been mounted, and books – including mine – have been written, but the mystery of Everett Ruess remains unsolved. No matter how many times the facts have been circled up, they all lead back to the beginning. Could it be that the mystery of Everett Ruess should remain unsolved? The truth is, Everett left us years before he disappeared. His was a slow disappearing act, like the Anasazi footpaths fading into the blue dusk.

After dark I do not build a campfire. Instead, I spread a tarpaulin and lay on my back, hands clasped behind my head. The silence and the starry sky calm me. At sunrise, I make my way to some high turrets of sandstone nearby and survey this fine prospect of wilderness. In my mind's eye, I can see the waves of heat shimmering off the super-heated surfaces of sandstone the first time I ventured into the intestine-like narrows of Davis Gulch in search of Everett Ruess.

AUGUST 1986

After carefully packing my daypack I start off for Davis Gulch less than a mile away. Few explorers are foolhardy enough to venture into the desert at this time of the year – and to hike alone, where a simple turned ankle can spell disaster, is taking an enormous risk. In my twenty years of wandering this red-rock canyon country, I have taken many calculated risks; this would be another. I am as prepared as anyone can be for all contingencies, or so I thought.

Davis Gulch was formed by water from rain and melting snow rushing off the mesa tops and cutting a deep, narrow gorge through the soft sandstone on its way to the Colorado River and now the man-made Lake Powell miles downstream. To get to Everett's last campsite, I will work my way down from the plateau top through the dangerous narrows of the gulch and then into the main canyon below. The narrows could present serious problems, yet once negotiated the gulch widens and becomes enchanting. The Anasazi Indians lived in the canyon bottom, as did old West outlaws wanting to make themselves scarce.

Before descending into the intestine-like narrows, I take a fix on my location. My reference point will be Fifty Mile Ridge to the west. Once in the deep canyon, it will be of no use to me, but somewhere below I will climb back out, locate my reference point, and make my way to it. I proceed with great caution. Some say the narrows are impassable, while others maintain that a strong agile person can make it. At first, the narrows are quite straight and I can see hundreds of feet ahead and behind me, but then slowly they narrow, finally corkscrewing and making cowlick-like turns where I can see only a few feet ahead or behind.

It is cool in the narrows, perhaps thirty degrees cooler than on the plateau above. Looking up, the sky is reduced to a blue ribbon running between the canyon walls hundreds of feet above. The passageway slowly closes in on me and at times I am forced to take my pack off, turn sideways and squeeze through. My breathing is labored, and it feels as if some heavy weight is pressing against my chest. Did Everett come this way, I wonder? What did he feel here?

Somewhere below, the narrows will widen and a year-round creek with lush greenery growing along its length will make this dangerous part of the hike worthwhile. From there, the narrows will be viewed as an adventure. This line of reasoning offers some comfort until rounding a corner I discover an enormous choke stone wedged across my path. The triangular-shaped boulder has fallen from the cliff top above and is wedged in such a way that there is no way to climb over it. There is, however, just enough room to squirm under it. A part of me wants to retreat, but I will not give in to my fears. Lying on my back in the sand, I shimmy under the ten-ton boulder's darkened mass. Sweat pools in my eye sockets. Fear tightens my chest. What if the boulder slips and crushes me? I can feel the weight of the stone on my chest. I struggle to breathe, but continue forward quickly.

Safely on the other side, I find no relief from the fear. Instead, I discover another obstacle: a twenty-foot drop-off with a plunge pool at the bottom. It is filled with stagnant primordial water and smells ghastly. I languish there far too long before wedging myself between the canyon walls, using a technique called friction climbing, and began working my way down. Halfway to the bottom, a horrible thought occurs to me; what if the pool of water is so deep it is over my head? Furthermore, if the narrows are really impassable, then the drop-off I am descending becomes a jump-up – a much more difficult obstacle to negotiate when coming back. With my back against one canyon wall and my hands and knees straining, I pause to consider my predicament. I have cast my lot; there is nothing for me to do but continue. At the bottom, I was happy to discover the pool is only knee deep.

For the next hour or so, I proceed slowly, working my way over and under choke stones, wedging my way down drop-offs and moving cautiously forward. The narrows widen a bit, arc to the left, then open into a long straight-away. I move forward to its end when suddenly I hear a voice! I freeze and strain to listen – nothing except my breathing and the pounding of my heart. Moving slowly forward, I hear it again. It is a voice, a human voice! It is growing clearer and coming up the narrows toward me.

"I'll bet no one has ever been this way before," a man's voice says.

I am stunned and respond without thinking, "Except for me, of course."

Silence.

"Anyone there?" I finally ask.

"Is someone up ahead of us?" a woman asks.

"Just lil' ole' me," I say, trying to sound friendly, but feeling annoyed. My adventure is devalued. I had traveled to one of the most remote and inaccessible places in North America and I faced dangerous predicaments for the purpose of being alone. Damn!

I hear other voices. They are low and heavy, like people discussing something of gravity. Finally, a man's voice rises up, "I just can't believe it!"

I lean against the sandstone and wait. A man appears in the narrow passageway ahead of me. He reminds me of Vincent van Gogh, had he lived to be seventy-five. Behind him is a woman about the same age. We exchange introductions. They are the Shaws, Don and Thelma, from California. Around the corner, hidden from view, are Helen, their daughter-in-law, and Katherine, a family friend.

They are vacationing with friends on Lake Powell some miles away.

It is difficult for me to fathom how this unlikely group of novices came to Davis Gulch. Even more perplexing is how they were able to climb up the narrows. I learn later it is their complete naiveté combined with Don's insistence that they continue that brought them to me. When Helen and Katherine finally come into view, I can see signs of fear and exhaustion in their faces. They are good looking, tanned and pampered; yet they are troubled and covered in scrapes and abrasions from head to toe.

For their part, they are incredulous that I am in the narrows alone, searching for some unknown poet who has been missing for nearly six decades. They advise me not to proceed. Glancing over her shoulder, Thelma says, "Mark, you'll never make it alone."

Don and I have a short discussion about what is on the plateau above. I suggest they turn around and we all go back down through the narrows and into the gulch. "It will be even more difficult getting back to the lake over the petrified sand dunes above," I say.

"I'll never go back there again!" Helen responds.

I was faced with my first real dilemma. If they are not going to follow me, I felt obligated to follow them, at least until I understood more about their plans. These people are not my responsibility. Still, with the intense heat and their unfamiliarity with the area, I believe they could be in serious trouble. It would be negligent, even criminal, not to assist them.

Two hours later, out of the narrows, we rest on a petrified sand dune resembling an enormous cow pie. Every year Don and Thelma vacation on Lake Powell, each time visiting another canyon or secluded alcove. Arguably one of the most beautiful lakes in the world, it has grown into a recreationalists' mecca. But it is highly unlikely that in today's environmental arena, the Glen Canyon Dam would have ever gotten off the drawing board.

Sitting around me on the sand dune this motley crew looks tired and thirsty. I offer them water, and they gulp it down greedily; they had been six hours without a drink. Then I offer them apples, cheese, crackers, and more water from my daypack. They are sunburned so I offer sunscreen, as well as Band-Aids and salve for their injuries. I give Don my extra shirt and pass Katherine the one I am wearing; she is in a bikini top and shorts. Her shoulders are already glowing with sunburn. My extra socks and sunglasses go to Thelma, but there was nothing I can do for Helen. She is wearing a pair of blue plastic slip-on shoes and no socks.

Her feet are red and swollen.

"They only cost me two dollars," she said.

I can't withhold my bewilderment any longer, "I can't believe you guys. You are totally unprepared. Look at me, I having hiking boots, water – fact is, you need a minimum of one gallon of water per person per day – I have food, rope, tools, and topographical maps. Whether you know it or not, hiking this country is very dangerous. If you aren't properly prepared, you're risking your life."

No one has the right to be unprepared, I say to myself. Yet, I am here alone – a sin of the highest order.

My outburst surprises them but they didn't act resentful. They seem unaware of the danger and do not fully appreciate my concern. Thelma explains that when they left the boat at 6:30 a.m. it was cool and they planned to hike only a few hours. "That's why we didn't bring anything with us," she says.

I sense that Don does not take what I say seriously. After all, why should he? I am out there alone, and if it is as dangerous as I make out, what am I doing here? Perhaps I am the one whose judgment should be questioned.

Thelma, Helen and Katherine are bone-tired, but surprisingly, Don (I was to learn later, a self-made millionaire) appears fresh and undaunted. Don's plan was to hike to the top of the gulch and then return via a trail he believes is on the plateau above. Don had been in the area once years earlier and is convinced a trail, located to the northwest, will lead them back down to the lake.

Don is incorrect and I tell him so. We consult my topographical map. It shows no trail. Still, Don insists it is there. I knew if they hiked northwest it would take them farther away from the lake and into a maze of sandstone formations known for swallowing up livestock. The sun-bleached bones of many desert-wise cattle litter the area – Everett's bones may well be among them.

Again, I attempt to convince these intelligent people to go back through the narrows. "It is the fastest and safest way," I tell them, but they would have nothing to do with it. One trip through the narrows was quite enough, thank you.

If Don has his way, there is an excellent chance they will join Everett somewhere out here. To complicate matters, they haven't grasped the tragic implications of their folly, so they don't ask me for help. I have no choice; I have to stay with them whether they want me to or not.

"If you're not going back the way you came, let me lead you back along the canyon rim." I pull out my map and with my finger follow the canyon ridgeline toward

Lake Powell. To my surprise, the women eagerly accept my offer. Don looks down at the sandstone and says nothing. I knew there was no path leading back to the lake as Don believed, and if they are not going to return the way they came, then following the canyon rim is the next best plan.

If they return via the narrows, it will mean another six-mile hike, but following the canyon rim and being forced to detour around intersecting canyons makes the return distance several miles longer. To make matters worse, they had already hiked many miles in the treacherous heat, and we have very little water left. I try to sell the narrows one more time, but it was no use. I have cast my lot and perhaps my life with this group of neophytes.

The path I pick is not easy, and our progress is slow and hard won. Time and again, we are forced to detour around deep, narrow tributary canyons intersecting Davis Gulch. Periodically, we stop to rest in the shade of rock outcroppings. We finish off the last of the water - it is hot but, oh, so delicious. As the others rest, I scout ahead, exploring the tributaries, hoping to find a quick and safe way down into the gulch.

Back on the trail, as a diversion I tell them how in March of 1935, after Everett had been missing for four months, a search party comprised of farmers from Escalante found his two burros in Davis Gulch. The animals were alive and well, and in a man-made corral. This offered hope that Everett would be found alive as well. Searchers followed his footprints along the canyon bottom. They located his campsites, found his tin cans, and even found a place where they believed he left a cryptic message scrawled into the soft sandstone wall. The message read: "NEMO was here. Nov. 1934" but Everett Ruess was not to be found.

The mystery became even more perplexing when searchers could not find his camp equipment and personal belongings. The authorities were stumped. Some speculated Everett was killed by a rustler or renegade Navajo who buried the body and took his belongings. Others theorized that he fell from one of the thousands of cliffs in the area and was never found. This theory has merit; in a letter to his brother, Waldo, in 1934, Everett wrote, *"Many times in the search for water holes and cliff dwellings, I trusted my life to crumbling sandstone and angles little short of the perpendicular, startling myself when I came out whole and on top."*

Those who believe Everett perished from a fall explain his missing belongings by maintaining that they are still out there somewhere. If these people are right, Everett's 1934 journal would be there, too. If his journal were found, it might offer clues to what happened to him. It would undoubtedly fetch a hefty price in the publishing business.

Still, there are others who believe that when the first two searchers from Escalante entered Davis Gulch, they quickly located Everett's camp and equipment. They could see that he had not been there for a long time and concluded he was not coming back. At that point, they divided his goods and kept quiet.

The Shaws and I march on mile after circuitous mile, detour after detour. The water is long gone. My mouth is so dry I try an old Boy Scout trick, sucking on a small pebble. I wouldn't advise it though; the soft sandstone disintegrates in the mouth. By late afternoon, the first signs of dehydration appear. Our pace slows to a crawl. Once, after a short rest, Don hiked off back the way we had just come. Another time, he points to a rock outcropping on the horizon and suggests we hike over to it and get a better look.

"But Don," I said, "between where we are standing and where you are pointing there is a canyon, hundreds of feet deep." I invite him to look at the map, which he does, but he still insists we can "just walk over there." I suggest he go take a look. When he returns he seems genuinely perplexed and admits there is indeed a canyon.

We enter into an area where freestanding spires and fins reach to the sky. It was difficult not to see the resemblance of these formations had to sexual body parts. Enormous phalluses jostle in position at the edge of huge breast-shaped domes with cleavages beckoning. Twisting rocks with fashionable posteriors, some with gaping vaginas or mooning rectums, invite further exploration. Even the fin-shaped formations are reminiscent of our once-aquatic erogenous apparatus; before this land was formed, we swam great oceans and our dorsals were a main attraction.

In July of 1935, after three quasi-official searches failed to solve the mystery of Everett's disappearance, ace reporter John Upton Terrell was dispatched from the Salt Lake Tribune to investigate. Because neither Everett nor his equipment had been found, many believed he was still alive. Some romantics theorized Everett married a beautiful Navajo maiden and was living in secrecy on the Navajo Reservation. Terrell enlisted help from three Navajos; one a famous tracker named Dougi, another a powerful medicine man, Natani, and his psychic wife. After chanting and praying, Natani told Terrell, "He (Everett) has gone away and does not mean to come back." Asked if that meant Everett was dead, the shaman responded, "There is a shadow and I do not see clearly. I only say that he has gone away, and he went from where he camped."

Dougi, who was already famous for tracking down

outlaws and desperados a generation earlier, traveled with Terrell to Davis Gulch and conducted his own search. After several days in the canyon and on the plateau above, Dougi was stumped. He had found many signs of Everett that had been overlooked by previous search parties. He found Everett's footprints miles away at the Hole in the Rock overlook and again at the base of Fifty Mile Ridge at the top of Davis Gulch. Dougi even found the exact place where, eight months earlier, Everett laid his bedroll for the last time. Still, no clear picture emerged.

He told Terrell, "Everett did not go south or east into Navajo land, and there is no sign of him going north or west."

"Could he have been killed and buried in Davis Gulch?" Terrell asked.

"No," Dougi said, "I would have easily found his grave."

As Don, Thelma, Helen, and Katherine shuffle along, I anxiously scout ahead. If I can just find a way into the canyon, our worries will be over. A vertical drop of only 300 feet separates us from water and safety. We are so close yet so far. When I return from one such scouting venture, I find Don, Thelma and Helen moving off to the northwest in the direction of Don's nonexistent trail. I assure them it can't be much farther, and if they follow me, I could guarantee success. Thelma and Helen look at me with relief, yet Don only reluctantly rejoins the group.

It is difficult for Don to relinquish control to me – or I suspect to anyone – perhaps as difficult as it would be for me to relinquish control to him. I am a reluctant participant in our little battle of the wills, but at this point I have a vested interest in the outcome.

After a particularly long and difficult stretch with the sun beating down unmercifully, the group rests and I explore yet another dangerous looking chasm nearly. I move quickly down a series of steep, dry, stair-like waterfalls, each with a plunge pool at the bottom – a total of perhaps 200 vertical feet. At the last plunge pool I find a 100-foot drop-off. There will be no getting into the gulch this way.

I turn and begin to climb back out when, to my utter horror, I discover I can't get out! In my haste, I had scurried down the steep rock face without thinking about climbing back out. Again and again, I throw myself against the nearly vertical walls, but each time I fall back – once, nearly plummeting off the cliff. Is this what happened to Everett, I wonder? My folly is compounded because I left my daypack with a rope inside with the others. I prepared for this day for years, but now that it is here, I find myself unprepared. My pack and its contents will be of no use to me. I yell to the others and wait, but no one comes. They have deserted me.

A half hour later, as I frantically notch footholds in the sandstone with the can opener on my Swiss Army knife, I hear Katherine calling for me.

"Down here!" I cry out.

Katherine retrieves my daypack and throws the rope down so I can hoist my dumb ass out. By the time we make it back to where the others should have been they are gone. I scramble to the top of a giant cow-pie formation and scan the horizon. I call out but only silence answers.

There is no time to waste. Without water there is little chance that Don, Thelma and Helen will make it. Katherine and I hike as quickly as the terrain allows. Earlier, I marshaled my energy but now it is time to go for broke. For more than two hours we keep up a grueling pace, covering a tremendous amount of country. Fatigue plagues us and we are desperate for water. The heat is excruciating. My arms hang like giant holiday hams from my torso and my legs burn to the marrow.

Finally, at the place where even good-natured people turn nasty, just before the juncture where exhaustion and defeat collide, an obvious path appears below leading us down into Davis Gulch.   I cry out, "Gawd Damn, we made it!" Katherine and I embrace.

Once in the cool canyon bottom, our hope is buoyed and we make tracks down the gulch to the lakeshore. I am dazed, light-headed and sick to my stomach. When we finally reach the lake we strip down and dive into the cool blue water. I have long resented this lake, but now it is sublime beyond measure. Within a few seconds, I cramp up and have to work hard just to climb out.

It has been twelve hours since Don, Thelma, Helen and Katherine left for a morning hike and the members of their party are frantic. When we arrive at their boat, Doug, Don and Thelma's son and Helen's husband, was preparing to hike up the gulch. If we had been ten minutes later, he would have hike four or five miles up Davis Gulch only to reach the narrows after dark.

It's 6:30 p.m., too late for the authorities to mount a search before nightfall, but not too late to climb back onto the plateau and make one last attempt to find them. I give Doug my map and pinpoint the place they might be if they continued in a northwesterly direction from where we separated.

Doug is drunk. He has marked the waiting time drinking highballs. Worse, his eyes swim across the features of the map and he admits, "I've never hiked in the desert before."

This is not good, but I say nothing. Doug's family is in grave danger and they need his help. I watch him start up the steep rock face leading to the plateau, carrying a gallon of water and a marine radio; as he went I wondered if he too, will become a victim. It's obvious Katherine and I suffer from exhaustion and dehydration, yet I promise to follow Doug onto the plateau after a little rest and rehydration.

A half hour later, I start my slow ascent up the switchback incline. I feel slaphappy from exhaustion and dizzy from the heat. I feel hollow too and fear I will pass out. One foot in front of the other, I kept telling myself. I also carry a gallon of water and a marine radio, and just as I reach the plateau above, Doug's excited voice comes over his radio. He has found his father wandering across the superheated, petrified sand dunes. At first, Don neither recognizes his son nor does he know where Thelma and Helen are.

When I arrive, Don is sitting on a large flat stone by himself. Doug has gone on ahead, attempting to locate the others.

"There was no trail," he admits as I approach.

I am angry and want to shout, I told you so! Don is

very weak, but assures me he will be all right, so I leave him with a gallon of water and move off into the desert.

It is dusk and the landscape is submerged in a hot, golden marmalade atmosphere. Large sandstone formations miles away appear closer than smaller ones just hundreds of yards away. The dusk is so beautiful and I'm transfixed, gazing out into the wild and unreal light. I have a strong desire to sit down and consider eternity. But tonight, eternity will have to wait; there is less than one hour to find Thelma and Helen and return to the lake. I push onward, every footfall feeling like ten.

It is a mistake for me to be here. My eyes are playing tricks on me. I see Everett standing at the bottom of a ledge, smiling up at me, but when I look again he is gone. I know my search for Everett has become more important than finding him. It is clear that Everett should remain missing and I should continue searching. The pursuit of his silhouette standing at the next horizon is fulfillment enough. I am on the right pathway.

Still, I push onward, my equilibrium impaired and my ability to make judgments gone. Doug's voice comes over the radio again; he has located Thelma and Helen, but something is wrong. He is frantic - his mother is unconscious. She laid down in the shade of a rock outcropping and now cannot be aroused.

Luckily, by the time I arrive Thelma is conscious again and sitting up. She suffers from exposure and disorientation. "You saved us, Mark!" she cries out when I appear on a hilltop. Thelma can't walk unassisted, so I put my arm around her and she puts her arm around me and we walk back together. Helen's feet are so badly injured from her plastic two-dollar shoes that Doug piggybacks her the entire way back.

That night I rest on an air mattress in the bow of Don and Thelma's quarter-million-dollar boat. I am exhausted, but sleep will not come. I watch stars sweep across the sky from horizon to horizon, in a race to infinity – a race where winners place dead last.

Someone approaches from the boat's stern. It is Don. Since returning to the safety of the boat, Don has been quiet – so quiet – in fact, everyone is worried, but no one – not even Thelma – ventures near him.

"Mark, are you awake?" he asks.

"Yes."

"I was wrong, Mark," he says in the halting manner of men of my father's generation who gag on such words as "sorry," "wrong," and "love."

I quickly get to my feet and we embrace. When I pull

back, I was startled by what I see. In the starlight Don has transformed into Achilles from Homer's Iliad. Tanned, bearded, and wearing a loose-fitting white muslin robe, Achilles stands before me. Don is ageless, like the stars.

The next morning long before the sun reaches into the canyon bottom I am on my way. I do not go back the way I came, choosing instead to skirt around the petrified sand dunes and make my way back to the road. From the plateau above, I measure the distance to my reference point Fifty Mile Ridge. It is many miles away. Standing there surveying the prospect of this land, I notice a faint trail to the northwest. Time and the elements have nearly obliterated it. Don had been right – there is indeed a trail. Unfortunately, the trail would not have helped my new friends. Later, I learn it is an Anasazi trail, perhaps the same one Everett followed on his way into eternity.

CHAPTER EIGHT

ROUND TABLE TWO

RIO VERDE

When Dr. Andbacka's office called on Friday to give me the results of the biopsy taken from my breast I was not available and would have to wait until Monday to receive the verdict. I flew back to Rio and spent much of the weekend in seclusion, considering the great struggle many women fight, sometimes winning and oft times losing the breast cancer battle. I have long admired the grace, poise, determination, stamina and hope that women often demonstrate when facing breast cancer.

At the same time I have known men of good character whose mission is to serve and give strength. I hope I have been one of these men. Because of my physical size and masculinity I've been viewed as steady and worthy of assisting those needing protection. I've liked this part of my manhood and I've faced tragedy straight up, offering what strength and solace as I could. I stood as a sentinel and delivered eulogies for the father I loved and respected just days after he died in my arms. I did it again when my best friend Mick shot himself in the heart; and then again when I could barely stand for my beloved mother whose separation will forever be an open wound. With my heart in my hand I tried to speak about who they were and about the pain of separation.

I've delivered a dozen eulogies and one of the first was for my oldest and dearest female friend Nancy Delafera. We grew up together and I played the role of her older brother and protector. She had been desperate to stay alive for her children, but alas she succumbed to liver cancer at age 38.

Nancy was petite, smart and very funny. She possessed a beguiling Siren's allure and needn't utter a word to be noticed. As a young man I looked away when we talked so as not to be entranced. Men young and old were captivated by her striking appearance and Madonna-like charisma. Nancy was soft spoken and refused to acknowledge the power she wielded as a woman and sexual divinity. When diagnosed and given six months to live, her tremendous life force kept her alive for nearly three more years.

After college she taught at-risk children and then went on to graduate school and landed a dream job teaching at Pepperdine University. She was an intellectual pow-erhouse and the world of opportunity blossomed for her. But a few months into her tenure she developed abdominal pains and x-rays and scans showed advanced liver cancer. She returned to Utah heartbroken where her friends and family closed rank around her.

Weeks before her death she and I went to a feminist play we loved, A – *My Name Is Alice*, and when I arrived at her door she was wearing a stunning white summer dress that accentuated her thick black hair, perfect olive com-plexion and radiating femininity. She weighed less than seventy pounds and could no long walk so at the theater I swept her up into my arms and carried her down the aisle like a Hercules or Odysseus and the room went silent as if in the presence of a deity. We laughed our heads off and af-terwards visited the cemetery where she now rests. Nancy wanted to visit the grave of our friend Sylvia Knight who had been taken by a drunk driver the night after she was crowned Homecoming Queen at our high school. It was a warm evening and we lounged on the luxurious grass atop Sylvia's plot and spoke of the joy of living. After a while we fell silent and watched the night clouds pass across a full moon.

Monday morning I leave the house for my doctor appointment telling Lana not to worry and that everything – no matter what the outcome was – would be okay and we would continue as we had for the last three years. Driving the low rolling hills covered with Purple Sage and occasional Mesquite and Saguaro trees I am overwhelmed by anxiety. I can't breathe and feel I might suffocate. I gulp back the emotion rising up from my chest and wonder where I might find the strength to comfort and console those who love me. I need to be strong and the force of nature I've always been. Talking out loud, I practice the uplifting speech I will recite for Lana when I get home with the bad news. I worry the strength I've depended on will fail me before the end. Before my father died he would take my arm when no one was watching and allow me to guide him, to help him down steps and be a silent partner in his manhood. Who can I find who will do that for me?

ROUND TABLE

Suddenly a wave of light-headedness sweeps over me. The sound of the car and highway slip away and my arms and legs are numb and won't work. Nothing seems important and the only thing I feel is my heart beating and air coursing in and out of my lungs.

The next thing I know I am no longer driving, but

floating in a space filled with soft and warm colors and I have the feeling I've been here before. It is the place of beginnings and endings.

"Marcus," a woman calls out to me.

"Someone there?" I ask, searching the emptiness.

"What color is the wind?" the woman asks.

"What color is the wind?" Then it comes to me.

"Nancy! Is that you?"

"Yes, Marcus."

The only person to ever call me Marcus was my best friend Nancy. Just before she died, on a lazy afternoon, we talked about Zen Buddhism and she queried me about the color of the wind.

"Oh, Marcus my darling, yes we are all here – for you."

I begin to sob uncontrollably and I'm unable to see through the tears I've held back for so long now. My chest heaves and a knot of emotion fills the back of my throat and nearly closes it off. My head hurts from pressure.

"Mark!" a man's voice demands, "Can you hear me? It's me, Randall.

"Remember me, your friend, Randall Potts?"

"Randall! Is it… really you? You've been gone for so long… Randall!… I thought you were gone…." I stop blubbering and swallow back tears.

"Oh, of course he is here," Nancy answers. "We are all here, do you think we'd forget you in your time of need? We love you Marcus, as you love us."

"I've always been here," Randall says. "I heard your questions, but I felt you knew the answers so I kept quiet."

And with this I realize I've been holding court with my dead friends for years now. I've spoken to each scores of times and they have answered me. I've even written about this personal other world, calling it the round table of my inner dialogues.

I am now standing in a large room with hardwood floors and a round table surrounded by empty chairs.

"Sweet Marcus," Nancy explains, "you don't know how we've missed you and how we've wanted to repay you for the love and help you offered us in our time of crisis."

"Oh please help me, Nancy," I beg, "I don't know what to do or where to turn."

Another voice speaks up, "If it ain't Potato Head Taylor. Fuck you."

"Same to you, fuck nuts," I answer. It is my friend Mick Tripp. I would know his voice anywhere. He and I have talked many times through the years.

"You are one lucky son-of-a-bitch," he starts telling me when Randall interrupts,

"Mark, I want to thank you for all of us. You gave us your strength, remember?" Randall's voice is deep and sweet and manly.

"Yeah, that goes for me, too," Mick adds, "You saved my as… and now you've made me famous…"

"Marcus, you were there for me during the moments of deep sadness." Nancy goes on, "And when my time came and I was on my death bed you wanted to steal me away. Remember? You were going to take me in your arms and outside to watch that very last sunrise - together."

"Oh, Nancy. I loved you so…"

"Do you remember befriending me?" Randall adds in. "I had no friends and you saw something in me that no one else saw – I couldn't even see it – and because of your faith I found myself. I never told you that…"

"We stand with you – at your side – as you did for us." Nancy comforts.

"Each of us faces our mortality in our own way," Randall says. "You can't see it right now, but you are finding your way…"

CHAPTER NINE

RIO VERDE

Days later, I was still shaken by what had happened. I wondered about Mick's comment that I had made him famous. I do remember in the months after his suicide I wrote an essay about him and what he meant to me entitled, "Say Something Pretty." It was featured in Utah Holiday Magazine and was subsequently picked up by United Press International and reprinted around the country.

In a way, the essay was a turning point for me as a writer. For the first time I employed a first person narrative. It was the first sign I might develop into a literary writer, rather than a journalist. The essay found a national audience and touched many readers. I received stacks of letters from people who had experienced the loss of a loved one to suicide. I was invited to speak to survivor groups and felt the despair suicide brings to loved ones. It's been years since I've read this essay and until recently I didn't even have a copy of it in my files.

SAY SOMETHING PRETTY

1984

It happened last February. A February I'll never forget. In what proved to be one of the worst winters in Utah history, a blitzkrieg of severe snowstorms christened the Siberian Express repeatedly bombarded the Wasatch Front. The once white and festive Christmas Eve snow – a window dressing for the wishful season - had compressed and hardened into a frozen granulated wafer, sandwiched neatly and unobtrusively between other express deliveries.

The snowy footpath leading from the parking lot to our apartment doorstep and to the doorstep of our next door neighbor, my oldest friend and confidant, Michael (Mick) Tripp was piled two feet deep on either side. It re-minded me of the luge competition I'd been watching on the Winter Olympic coverage from Sarajevo, Yugoslavia – but that was before Mick committed suicide.

At approximately noon on Monday, February 20, 1984, Michael L. Tripp, age thirty-three, a man whose life had been punctuated by bouts of severe depression, a series of unsuccessful attempts at taking his life, a profusion of psychiatrists, psychoses and mental health workers, took a cab downtown, bought a high-caliber handgun, went to a popular private club located on East 3900 South and shot himself through the heart.

Why did he do it? Why does anyone opt for suicide?

The truth about my friend is that he suffered from acute depression. He described it as a spiraling depression that, like a giant drainpipe, sucked him down. Mick was a serious, intelligent and sensitive man. His sensitivity was undoubtedly his greatest gift, but at the same time it was a contributing factor to his unhappiness.

It's impossible for me to write about Mick without writing in contradictory terms. He was an angry man, but an individual who displayed kindness and compassion. He enjoyed life, he knew how to laugh, but he derived an enormous amount of pain from living. He was a strong man, yet sometimes his strength rendered to weakness and he felt totally inadequate.

Mick fought what I can best describe as an internal war with conflicting inner dialogues, a battle that gave him little peace. To have seen him during one of these depressions was to see a man submerged in personal turmoil, anguish and pain.

As in many suicides, the seventy-two-hour period preceding his death was a personal nightmare. During this time he suffered from three of the four clinically identified triggering mechanisms associated with suicide. The four include depression, a personal crisis – such as the loss of a loved one or a sudden impulse, the use of drugs and alcohol, and finally, old age or disease – including the loss of his youth. I believe had he been able to defuse these mechanisms, he would be alive today. I desperately want to believe that.

On Friday night, February 17th, Mick started his last weekend with a violent argument with his girlfriend of three months. The upshot of the disagreement was that she wanted to date other men and was not ready for an exclusive relationship. To Mick the idea of an exclusive relationship was part and parcel to his overall image of personal success and happiness.

After several mixed drinks, he left in his automobile. He drove to Parley's Canyon where he rolled his car and was arrested for driving under the influence. Early Saturday morning he was released from the Salt Lake County jail on his own recognizance. He then tried to admit himself into the psychiatric unit of the University Medical Center. He was turned away because no bed was available. He ended up at Pioneer Valley Hospital in West Valley City. Four hours later he was released to the custody of his mother, but not before they injected him with Demerol, a drug he had a history of abusing.

Saturday night and Sunday the 19th he spent alone in his apartment. I know this because Margo, my wife and I could hear him playing the same record over and over again. It was an old album by America, one that contains a song entitled "Ventura Highway" – a whimsical song about living a carefree life on the road. He never played that album unless he was depressed and wanted to remember the "good old days."

I knew something was wrong, but I didn't want to hear about it. There came a time years earlier when I had to disengage from his depressions and talk of suicide for the sake of my own mental health. In recent years he very seldom turned to me during these times. I don't regret this; it was the way it had to be. On two occasions, more than ten years earlier, I had found him unconscious from drug overdoses and had carried him over my shoulder into the emergency room. A doctor at the hospital told me, "You saved his life. If you hadn't brought him in when you did, he would have died."

It was snowing and well below zero Sunday night when Margo and I, accompanied by our Doberman, Bask, knocked on Mick's door to ask if he wanted to go for a walk in the park near our house. He didn't answer. Through his plate glass front door we saw his shadow, cast by his bedroom light, move across the semi-dark living room floor. I realize now, the last time I saw my friend, I didn't really see him; I only saw his shadow.

In the days and weeks following his death – until the weather broke and the snow melted – that snowy footpath, made in part by Mick, haunted Margo and me. His last footprints, leading inexorably into eternity, greeted us every morning and welcomed us home each night. Somehow his footprints tormented us and gave us great comfort at the same time.

Today, eight months later, on cool autumn evenings when Margo and I sit in our patio grotto, one we shared with Mick for two years, I miss him more than words can express. Sometimes I can hear his voice; it's as though he was right there with us. Other times his voice is muffled and I suddenly feel desperate that I'll lose its sound forever.

I still find myself talking out loud to him. I chide him for his insensitivity to us. I tell him it's a good thing he's gone because if he were here, right now, I'd punch him in the face. I still admonish him, after all this time, to come back, to abandon this practical joke and return to us. Although the snow is gone, I still see that icy footpath every time I look toward his front door. I dread the thought of the oncoming winter.

In my daydreams, while I'm driving, I still devise ways he could have avoided death. If just one element of his suicide equation was missing, or another added, he might be here with us today. I tell him we love him dearly and ask how he'd feel if I was the one who took his life. How would he feel burying me? I still find time to cry.

It was high school in the late 1960s in Salt Lake City when Mick and I became friends. After graduation, like tens of thousands of other kids of our day and age, we set out to find America. In six months we chalked up more than 25,000 miles hitchhiking and freight train riding. We ended up in northern Minnesota, working as loggers and living on an organic dairy farm owned and operated by devotees of the Rosicrucian Fellowship of the Cosmic Conception. During that carefree summer, we forged a friendship that survived more than fifteen years. Even though there were times we lived in different cities or states, we always kept in touch. In all those years, Mick never forgot my birthday. I wish I could say the same.

Mick would have graduated from nursing school in June of this year. Just four days before his death, the last time we really talked, he told me was planning to buy a

Harley-Davidson motorcycle – Harleys were salvation on wheels to him. He told me he wanted to lose weight and get back into shape because, according to him, he was thirty-three years old and felt he had at least thirty-three more. I'm convinced Mick wanted to live.

Another truth about my friend is that he had a death wish. He thought of his own demise often. The option of ending his pain was with him always. It might sound morbid, but he and I discussed his death. As the years passed I tried to avoid these conversations. He talked about how disgusted he was with life and himself and how he always fell short of his own expectations. I talked about handicapped people and individuals who were much worse off than I considered him. Less than one month before his death, during one of these conversations when he was telling where he wanted his possession to go, I said, "I'll bet you want me to speak over your dead carcass too, when you go, right?" He smiled and answered, "Say something pretty."

For me, when I reach my inevitable acceptance, I'll remember Mick for his truly remarkable memory. He was my memory for the times we spent together. I'll remember his compassion for the underdog and the thoughtfulness and consideration he always showed me. And finally, I'll never forget the times he came to my assistance. He was always there when I needed him. I'll miss that most.

For Mick and me, for the time we spent together, I somehow learned things first. I was the one with all the luck. I was the one who got the girl and who was asked to all the parties. Somehow I always knew the story's ending before he did. But this time Mick learned the truth about life's greatest mystery first.

"Hey Mick, what are we looking at?"

CHAPTER TEN

CLEARWATER, FLORIDA

APRIL 2011

FORT HARRISON

I was hoping to avoid this but here I am again stuck in another groupthink meeting that has just droned past the three-hour mark. I feel I'm part of a Josef Stalin Communist Party loyalty test where audiences attending Stalin's endless speeches hold their seat and continue to clap after the speech concludes, fearful of the consequences of being the first to stop. Some audiences clapped for hours until they dropped from their seats asleep or exhausted.

When the next person starts to speak I slip away again, escaping momentarily into the rich oil painting of church founder, L. Ron Hubbard on the far wall of the conference room. I can just imagine it now, the swank LA Celebrity Center auditorium filled with dazzling Hollywood Scientologists dressed in designer gowns and tuxedos. There's

Tom Cruise and John Travolta and Tommy Davis and his gorgeous mother, the actress Ann Archer! The crowd is on its feet giving David Miscavige a standing ovation. And it goes on and on until the autonotoms' clapping becomes herky-jerky,- each person loathe to be the first to stop the adulation, fearful of what message it might convey.

What would Mr. Hubbard think of Miscavige now, his one-time manservant and pre-ordained successor, the man who recreated his church in his own Hollywood likeness?

But enough day-dreaming. As the only civilian and non-high ranking Scientologist present at the Fort Harrison conference table, I shift from one gluteus maximus to the other, activating my sphincter and practiced kegels. I check my smart phone, gather my materials, and wait for the current bloviator to relent. When the opportunity arrives, I push back from the table, straighten myself up and get to my feet.

"Sorry folks, it's getting late – and my rear-end can't take any more. Pardon me, but I've got to get some dinner and make a few calls."

A collective gasp of relief goes up, followed by a moment of all-smiles. I am the loser. Each has outlasted me – proof of what it means to be *Clear* or on the *Bridge*. For Scientologists, eye contact speaks truth, and each set of eyes offers me a thank you - for the audacity of calling it quits. These same eyes follow with an embarrassed eyelash flutter, a sympathetic acknowledgment of my innate inability to persist. They could have gone on forever.

With the spell broken, each participant checks their pagers or crackberries. One beautiful wife says, "Oh goodness, it's late. Got to get home to make dinner." At the doorway, I see her husband standing in the opulent lobby. Ben Shaw, my handler and Director of the Office of External Affairs, offers me a dry smile and a half-hearted dinner invitation to one of the hotel's first-class restaurants. I decline and escape to my room.

After spending a few hours online researching Paul Tash, the publisher of The Tampa Bay News and Joe Childs, its editor-in-chief, I decide I'll start with the basics. I'll tail each man for a week or so and see where they go and what they do when not working.

Later, unable to sleep, I pace my luxurious suite, desperate to stop the creepy feeling that I'm being watched – that my every movement is being recorded. I search my room again for eavesdropping technology, disassembling the telephone, clock radio and TV remote. I pull the plug on the television, remove the air conditioner covers, inspect the vents and stand atop a chair and take a close look at the light fixtures.

This is not the first time I've felt like a specimen or prisoner at Fort Harrison. My hink-o-meter redlined on my first visit to the palatial Flag – the spiritual hive of the Church of Scientology.

Exiting my rental car at the Flag entrance, Alexandro, the ever - friendly Italian bellman from Verona, rushes to welcome me to the Mediterranean Revival, VIP Fort Harrison hotel. Taking my bag, he leads me from the portico through the doorway, up some marble steps into the ornate nineteenth century lobby.

"Is it true," I ask, pausing to take it all in, "did Mick Jagger and Keith Richards write, I Can't Get No Satisfaction, here?"

"Yes sir," he points up, proudly, "in the penthouse."

Alexandro is Sea Org (Sea Organization) as are all staffers of Fort Harrison. Before this assignment he spent five years on the yacht Freewinds. Only the most fervent Sea Org members get that kind of assignment.

Alexandro directs me to the front desk and introduces me to Katrina, the sexy Russian front desk manager. He then disappears around a corner, taking my bag with him.

I'm surprised that Katrina knows who I am.

"Mr. Taylor," she says with a sharp Russian accent, "Welcome to Fort Harrison."

"Thank you."

As I fill out the check-in documents, Katrina phones the house doctor and hands me a medical questionnaire.

"Doctor?"

"Standard procedure," she flashes a Port of Vladivostok wintery smile.

The questionnaire includes personal questions I find intrusive so I pass it back to her.

"You haven't answered all the questions," she challenges.

"Right," I yawn impassively.

I learn later that after a guest mysteriously died at the hotel a few years back, resulting in a police investigation, a lawsuit and allegations of wrong-doing leveled by the Tampa Bay Newspaper, a policy requiring guests to fill out a health form and be interviewed by a doctor was instituted at check-in.

Laura, the Australian house doctor, arrives and we sit on an oversized leather couch. After a few questions, we have a good time visiting about the hotel and Florida's beautiful weather.

Back at the front desk I enquire,

"My bag?"

"It will be delivered to your room," Katrina says, pushing an envelope containing my electronic key across the marbled counter, "Room 912." She calls another bellman to take me up.

In the elevator, I ask, "What happened to my bag?"

"Your bag?" He responds, "I'll check when I get back to the lobby."

An hour later, Alexandro arrives with my bag and apologies for the delay. I think nothing more of the incident until I open the bag and sense that something is wrong – someone has gone through my luggage! Its contents appear to have been moved or rearranged, but I can't be certain. Why would someone go through my bag? After a thorough check, I conclude nothing is missing.

A month or so later on my next visit, the same scenario played out again. Alexandro disappeared with my luggage and when I enquired to Katrina, she responded with a Siberian permafrost how-dare-you look. But this time I made sure to remember the location of everything when I packed. When my bag finally arrived I couldn't say with any degree of certainty that it had been opened. Was it just me? Had I fallen prey to my own paranoia? But even if I had, what the fuck were they doing keeping my bag for an hour?

On my third visit, I refused to relinquish my bag and told Alexandro, "No need, I'll carry it myself."

After several charming, yet increasingly aggressive attempts to convince me to surrender it, he became agitated and his expression turns dark. The Brazilian Concierge rushes to intercede, asking if he could help. Bowing from the waist, he grabs my bag and tries to pull it away.

"I beg your pardon!" I say indignantly, holding tight. "I'll carry my own bag, if you don't mind."

We engage in a pull and push struggle.

"How come every time I'm here," I enquire loudly, "someone disappears with my luggage?"

He releases the bag, steps back and demurs, "Anything you say, sir. Just trying to be helpful."

I'd struck a nerve.

At the front desk, Katrina is wild with anger. Placing my bag down next to me, I maintain a cordial exterior, but when I am momentarily distracted, another bellman, Gabriel, a handsome young Spaniard, slips in beside me and tries to relieve me of it.

"What are you doing?" I demand, stepping in front of him.

"Excuse me, sir. Just trying to be of service."

"Your name?"

"Gabriel, sir."

"Thanks, Gabriel. I'll carry my own bag."

"Of course, sir," he smiles. "Next time you need anything, just ask for Gabriel. Just think of the archangel, Gabriel, from the bible, and you will remember my name."

"Will do."

I find it odd that a Sea Org member is referencing the bible.

Across the lobby, the concierge, Alexandro, and two security men watch and talk among themselves.

Scientologists, at least Sea Org members, chafe with irritation at the idea that the church is secretive or suspicious of outsiders. They see themselves as open and inviting. It is ironic then that Flag is a walled-in fortress. The hotel complex takes up an entire city block and is ringed by an imposing security wall. Everyone enters and exits through the same small portal. Staffers and inconspicuous blue-coated security officers populate this passageway around-the-clock. No one comes or goes without them knowing.

Since I can't sleep or shake the feeling I'm being watched, I decide to go on the offensive and test hotel security.

Five minutes before each hour, security makes its rounds on my floor. I hear the elevator door open and close, followed by footsteps moving past my door to the emergency fire exit at the far end of the hall. The door opens and closes quietly, and for a faint moment, I hear footsteps descending the stairs.

At 3:05 a.m., ten minutes after the last security sweep, I slip out and down the hallway to the stairs. One flight of steps after another, I descend following exit signs until I reach a security door labeled Restaurant and Parking garage. On its opposite side is a hallway leading right or left. In the distance, someone is operating a vacuum or floor polisher. If the door closes behind me it will lock, so I place a folded napkin under the door's corner and wedge it slightly open.

To the right I find the parking garage door securely locked. The other direction, I discover a stairway and at its bottom are restrooms marked Employees Only. I hear voices. The sound is trailing off so I continue to an open doublewide doorway leading into one of the hotel's kitchens. The room is tile and stainless steel and filled with rows of tables, stacked with cooking pots, mixing bowls and trays of silverware. A walk-in freezer is just a few feet away. The delicious aroma of baking bread and roasting meat fills the room.

This must be The Hour Glass restaurant's kitchen, located below the mezzanine near the hotel entrance.

Suddenly from behind, someone exits a restroom and is moving my way. I dash into the walk-in freezer and gently let the door close behind me. Luckily, a light activates so I'm not in the dark. As I crouch down behind a stack of boxes labeled potatoes the cooler's light goes out and I'm left in the cold blackness. I suspect Katrina would feel at home here. The freezer's motor obliterates all other sounds.

I wish I had a Scientologist's patience and perseverance, but I make up for it with audacity, a quality strangely absent or sequestered in them. At the point when I cannot take the cold any longer, I locate the door handle in the darkness and nonchalantly push my way out. If discovered I decided to say I had an unrelenting case of midnight munchies and decided to sneak into the restaurant to find food. Somehow, I'd taken a wrong turn and ended up in the freezer. Luckily, my gambit worked and no one was there.

Sneaking into the darkened dining room I spot the restaurant's glassed-in entranceway just beyond the hotel lobby. Two security men are standing at the top of the portico stairway. Someone is working in the kitchen behind me so I take refuge in a circular shaped booth, lying down on the plush leather seat. From my vantage point, I can watch security in the foyer and scan the entrance to the kitchen. My smart phone reads 3:30 a.m. It's been twenty-five minutes since leaving my room, but seems much longer.

A few minutes later, the security men disappear. Cautiously, I leave my hiding place and try to push through the restaurant's glass front doors. Locked! I have a clear shot at the hotel entrance just a few feet away but I can't get out. Back at my booth, I stretch out and consider my options.

A half hour later, a sound wakes me and I see a silhouette standing outside the glass front door. The person is fumbling with keys and looking for the right one to open the door. It's Stephen, the night auditor and front desk manager. Stephen has helped me when I've had an early flight and needed to check out. After finding the key, he goes to the cash register and runs out a paper tape of the previous day's receipts. Someone from the kitchen emerges and they small talk for a few minutes, then both disappear into the kitchen.

This is my chance! On tiptoes I make a dash for the front glass doors, scanning up into the lobby and down towards the hotel entrance. It really doesn't matter at this point, I've committed to this course.

Out through the restaurant's glass doors, down the marble steps and out the front door. I am free.

Liberated!

Chapter Eleven

RIO VERDE

Last night I wrote an email to a good friend and confidant, Ron Godfrey:

Dear Ron,

How goes it? I wanted to write and update you on what's happening here. I was being treated for a serious skin cancer condition and undergoing treatment including Mohs surgery, when quite by chance, a large mass was discovered deep in my left breast tissue. It hurt like hell to touch. It was breast cancer and I underwent surgery to have the tumor removed. The good news is it was caught early before it spread and I dodged a bullet on this one. The bad news is in the run up to the operation the doctors did a full blood panel and discovered my PSA was off the chart. A week or two later I was diagnosed with metastatic prostate cancer. It has already spread throughout my body and the tumors have metastasized into bone cancer and are now growing unchecked.

Ron fires back a response, "That's the shits, Mark. I'm so sorry. What are you going to do with the time you have left - write about it?"

That is the question: What am I going to do? For years I quoted J.R.R. Tolkien. He wrote: "There is only one important question known to mankind: What are you going to do with the time that has been allotted to you?"

My mental health is shot, one minute I'm a paper tiger showing my sharpened fangs and the next I'm a defeated, crumpled up wad of Kleenex filled with snot and tears. I've believed I could write about any subject, but I'm having a hell of a time mounting this challenge. I sit down to write and hours later I haven't moved or accomplished a thing. I feel paralyzed and have no interest in documenting *my* dying process. I understand as an artist this is where the meat, the action, and the power *is* but I'm so burdened I can't yet find the bottom of it. I'm not sure I have *this* narrative in my toolbox.

Mankind has produced optimists and philosophers whose ideas about death are based on facing death with a positive view. I even collect quotes about dying from great thinkers knowing I might need these powerful kernels some day when my time arrived. I would use them to combat the morose thoughts I knew I'd encounter. This makes some sense because I've seen a woeful parade of my loved ones and acquaintances make cameo appearances on the obituary page of the Salt Lake City Tribune.

I've even started my own obituary. I begin with an Old Russian proverb about death, "The bell tolls, a dog barks and the caravan rolls on."

Meanwhile as I attempt to understand my situation, I realize at my core I'm a misanthrope, someone who has a love/hate (mostly hate) relationship with humanity. The truth about humanity is we are a locust-like species. Right now we are masticating our way through the resources and substance of this planet and bringing untold pain, suffering, cruelty and death down on all other species, as well as each other. We have no regard or compassion for anything other than our current vacuous temporal needs. We justify our actions with silly notions of superiority and we are loath to acknowledge any responsibility for what we sow. When we have destroyed everything, we will turn on each other because that is our nature, and we will finally reap the reward we justly deserve.

Sitting at my writing desk in my studio I finally understand there are subjects that are so deeply meaningful I may never be able to write about them. I've fooled myself into thinking one day I would be able to speak with authority about such matters as love and death - to eloquently express my love for my mother and what it feels like to miss her and need her love and comfort. Or about the sons I sired, but did not father and who I rejected as men because they refused to honor me in the way I honored my father and he honored his father. I deserved more from them.

If I could I would speak with power about the love I was gifted, possessed and lost. I would celebrate the smart and sensitive and dear women who saw something in me, but who came and went because I had no room for them in my self-centered set of priorities. I set myself apart as undeserving and a pathetic and inadequate partner. I was married and divorced as an adolescent and the mistakes I made still haunt me and have somehow handicapped my ability to do as our hero Paul McCartney implored, "Let It Be."

Right now, I have several unfinished manuscripts in my filing cabinet and each is worthy of my time. I'm not sure I will ever get to them, but one in is calling out to me. It's the story about the disappearance of a best-selling writer who went missing without a trace. His name is David Thomson. I think I'll pick up his trail again while I still can.

Chapter Twelve

Roper Rail Yard

Salt Lake City, Utah

Summer 2018

Shading my eyes from the afternoon glare, I trace the well-worn path as it snakes down through a garbage-strewn field behind a line of old industrial buildings and leads into the transient camp. The camp is hidden below a freeway overpass and nestled against a stand of box elder trees on the bank of the Jordan River.

Returning to this hobo jungle is a homecoming for me and as I survey its nasty squalor, all the lost and forgotten images of this place load into my consciousness. In a strange conjunction of time and space, my recollections of this place and the reality are remarkably similar. This strikes me as odd because after so much time my memory usually re-jiggers reality, changing the physicality of places in some obvious or oblique way. It often adds a long-distilled romantic or dreamy elixir to a place as well. But here I am, more than thirty years removed, and my memories and the reality are remarkably the same.

Every square meter of this sad terminus has been pissed-on, shit-on, puked-on and fucked-on by one generation of missing people after another. Today, it's all consecrated ground and has an asphalt-like surface flecked with thousands of shards of broken glass. The sun dapples down through the box elders and the hard-packed surface sparkles like magic.

For a moment I am transported away, back to a night when Mick and I rode an empty DF freight car across Nevada with a group of drunken Navajos. It was hot that summer night and an argument turned into a fight and an empty wine bottle was thrown against the boxcar's wall, exploding into a thousand dangerous diamonds glistening in the moonlight.

Luckily, the train slowed into Winnemucca and we grabbed our gear and jumped out into the unattached darkness. For years afterwards, we chortled about this incident, picking it apart, putting it back together again - and it took its rightful place on the mantle of personal myth. The last time Mick and I laughed about it was during an intimate moment at a dinner party the night before he took his life. Funny how we cherish the dangerous experiences of our youth, but fail to see the face of present-day travails with any degree of clarity.

It feels good to get away from the studio and back on Dave Thomson's trail. I'll meet my Scientology deadline and feel good about it. Deep inside though, I know that time is running out for me and I need to recalibrate and get back on track to accomplish the work and goals I've set out for myself.

At the center of camp is a large fire pit with four overturned five-gallon plastic paint cans sitting around it. I plop down onto one without taking my pack off. The can's raised edge cuts into my butt but I choose not to acknowledge it. I'm just glad to be here alone - to have the desolation of this place to myself. Sitting atop a nearby can is a piece of art – a stick figure girl made from a discarded hypodermic syringe, a cigarette filter skirt and paper-book match arms and legs. Quite fetching.

Moments later, a part of me is on the verge of an important announcement. Ushering up from the murky internal sea, my chest expands and empties, and I feel light-headed and tearful. What ancient injury or current dilemma has decided this is the moment to step forth and make its existence known?

Who cares what the oncologist said about the breast or prostate or skin cancer? I'm nothing more than a cancer grow box, a fertile human medium or host for tumors and lesions. I am alive here and now. It is all any of us have. I recall what someone once said, 'In comparison to how long we will be dead, life is truly short, so let it play out and live while you are alive.'

Suddenly to my left, I spot a man hunkering down under the freeway overpass at the top of the steep cement abutment. He is draped in a sleeping bag and his legs are pulled up to his chest with his arms wrapped around them. His head is lowered, buried into his center. Ringlets of thick black hair crest into a top notch, reminiscent of a slumbering bear. Even from this distance, I can tell he is a giant.

On the other side of camp, in a coffin-shaped divot of dirt, a pile of old clothing is strewn about. At its center I see what appears to be the shape of a human form. Standing up, I move closer to get a better look, thinking it might be a dead body. I venture, "Hey, you okay?"

The form rolls over to face me and raises one arm behind his head for a prop.

"What're yew lookin' at?" he asks.

"Just checking."

The man is about sixty-years-old, filthy and skinny.

"Where's my fucking cigarettes?" he searches the pile.

"Don't look at me."

"You take em?"

He is not really talking to me.

After finding his smokes he seems satisfied until he realizes something else is missing.

"My hat?"

A greasy Oakland Raider's cap hangs upside down, suspended in the dried June grass nearby. Scratching his torso with both hands, he searches the pile.

"There," I point.

He shoots a hateful glance and as he does, I see the whites of his eyes are yellow. He tries to stand but falls back, so instead he crawls through the weeds to retrieve the hat. He trembles and his forehead, back and chest are covered in droplets of sweat. I turn away and mind my business.

Roper Rail Yard is just a few hundred yards to the south. A line of four-thousand-horse-power diesel engines idle on one of many tracks nearby - vibrating the ground and creating a deep industrial hum. Over the years at night, as I sprawl in my comfortable bed listening to the blast of locomotive whistles coming from far off distant places, I longed to join them, to disappear into the darkness and rejoin the cavalcade of the lost and intentionally missing.

I take in a deep breath and savor the yard's bouquet. Once you get a taste of it, you'll never forget it. It is a combination of diesel fumes, solvents, burning machine oil and slag. Spend enough time around a rail yard and you'll long for the way the chemicals burn in your throat and its gritty bite coats your tongue and teeth.

With dusk approaching, travelers filter into camp arriving in small groups. Three weary and ghost-like men arrive covered in fine soot, each carrying a gallon of water, a few belongings and a big piece of cardboard. The oldest has probably been at it since the end of the Vietnam War. Sprawling out under a tree, they pull out a gallon of cheap wine and make themselves at home. The letters, FTRA are tattooed in large blue and black letters on the older man's forearm, beneath a stylized red swastika. A man and woman arrive next, she looks frightened and both are drunk. Two young men arrive about the same time, one carrying a bucket of KFC (Kentucky Fried Chicken). They have no gear or water, and I learn later they are not here to catchout, but use the camp as a regular place to eat and sleep. They are workers from Mexico. One casts a nasty-MS13 - gang look around that says, 'Don't fuck with me, Asay.'

I pace back and forth at a distance, shadowboxing and speaking to an imaginary foe. I gesticulate too, pointing my fingers and throwing punches at the air. No one messes with a crazy fucker. In crazy environments, it's better to act a little nuttier than the rest.

On the other side of the rail yard in an empty field I spot a man crouching down near some bushes and a barbed wire fence. He cups a cigarette in his palm, taking deep drags and revealing high cheekbones and a furrowed brow. Someone is probably looking for him and he doesn't want to be found.

Back in the rail yard, a switching crew is building the westbound freight train. They pull cars from different tracks and push them together onto the main line. After attaching the diesel locomotive engines and connecting the air brakes, the train's departure won't be long now.

As dusk deepens the western sky fills with electric red. I feel energized – younger even. Like in the film, Repo Man, where one character points to a beautiful family getting out of a car and says to his sidekick, 'See those people? Normal people – fuck I hate 'em! Normal people spend their entire lives trying to avoid intense situations. But Repo Men, we spend our entire lives trying to get into intense fucking situations.' And that's how I feel right now, like a fucking Repo Man – alive in ways that my timid, static contemporaries will never know. I am ready for intense situations.

A dispute erupts in camp. A third member of the Mexican KFC crew arrives to discover his compatriots have eaten all the chicken breasts.

"Fucking sons-of-bitches!" he shouts, searching the bucket. "Fucking chicken-shit wings!"

He is inconsolable, kicking at the ground and holding his head as if it might explode. He shouts insults in Spanish and English. His rant is funny, and the soot-covered ghost riders are humored, sitting back with wine and hand rolled cigarettes.

KFC man takes a step back and then kicks the bucket of chicken like a soccer ball, launching it across the camp and scattering the drumsticks and chicken wings in the dirt. They are all on their feet now, moving in a clockwise circle, pushing and shoving. I move out of the camp, positioning myself near the mainline. I find a nice thick piece of cardboard where someone left it. I hope to find an empty boxcar for myself. I don't want to share the trip with any of this crew.

Struggling under the enormous weight, the huge locomotives come to life, drowning out all other sounds. The train inches slowly forward and this is my cue. It's now or never. Darting across the mainline in front of engines to the opposite side, I position myself where I can search for an empty boxcar with open doors. I need to find a one quickly, before the train catches so much speed I am unable to climb aboard.

About twenty cars into the train, I spot an empty, its doublewide doors open. The challenge is to run alongside the slow – moving train as it picks up speed until the open boxcar parallels you, then jump or launch yourself into it. As the car reaches me, I quicken my pace, throw my pack and cardboard inside and grab the door's railing with one hand and hold tight – a fall now can be deadly. When the time is right, I launch myself up into the car, landing the top half of my torso on the wooden floor, and quickly pull my legs in.

By the time I find my footing, the train passes the camp and I see the Latino men fighting. One has another in a headlock and the other is trying to punch and kick him.

Suddenly, the giant from the abutment appears in the open doorway. He is moving fast, running alongside, trying to match the train's speed. Grabbing the car's door runner he struggles to keep pace. He throws his sleeping bag aboard and readies himself for a leap. My first instinct is to kick his hand away, but I just stand there watching, trying to stay afoot and not fall out. Somehow, with the agility I would never have imagined a man his size could muster, the giant leaps and lands his enormous trunk into the car and pulls legs safely inside.

Turning to me with the amazed look of a child, he says, "Blacin soobal tota!"

"Right!" I exclaim.

Without another word, my riding companion retreats to the back of the boxcar, sitting in a corner, throwing the sleeping bag over his shoulders.

Once out of the freight yard, I sit in the open door and dangle my legs; I will let this exquisite experience flow over me and have its way. The memories of long-ago freight train rides dance in and out of my mind and mingle with this present moment. I see Mick's huge, toothy smile, and Penny's sexy eyes. This mix of past and present is exhilarating, but tinged with a longing and sadness - so much time has gone by, so many losses have mounted up.

Riding the rails offers up the backside view of urban life. The rundown shanties, the piles of used tires and discarded rolls of old carpet, the fenced-off lots filled with weeds and windblown trash, the gutted cars and junkyards and polluted waterways, the itinerate camps where the forsaken, lost and drug addled hunker down, and the places where broken down dreams go to die.

The tracks cross roadways where warning lights flash, alarm bells sound and impatient motorists sit and wait. I feel like a child riding an amusement park attraction without a ticket; waving occasionally at someone sitting in a car, flipping people off, and feeling smug in my vagabond's coat and trousers. This is an adventure few will ever know and money cannot buy. At some invisible line of demarcation, I pass out of the conventional and into a parallel world of the underground; always in transit, always gyrating and never lamenting what should have been done.

Out past the Great Salt Lake, the train opens up and races across the Bonneville Salt Flats toward Nevada. To the east, a full moon peeks over the receding Wasatch Mountain Range and the new moonlight catches in the crystalline salt and creates a sea of shimmering light. I hear the voice of Ram Dass – *Be Here Now, Be Here Now*. And I am fully here right now, in this fleeting yet recursive moment.

In this moving sea of light, the feeling of homecoming returns. The clacking of the steel wheels as they cross the joints in the metal track; the methodical rocking of the boxcar; the wind circulating inside this creaking and moaning box of wood and steel. I push back from the doorway and lay on my cardboard bed. I want to savor every moment of this ride. At the southern horizon, a string of headlights a mile or two away mark Interstate-80 and the many lives coursing along its narrow strip of asphalt.

Riding the rails makes you free. People who ride the rails don't punch time clocks, pay mortgages, worry about IRAs, or take on ill-fitting jobs and lifestyles that lead to boredom and a feeling of worthlessness. Riders don't care about getting ahead or getting their share of electronic devices or material goods.

A few years back, while working as a magazine editor I met a colleague after work for drinks. After hammering down one drink after another and taking turns bemoaning how misunderstood our talents were or how poorly paid we were, a man outside the window on the sidewalk caught our attention. He was about our age and looked pretty much like we did, but this guy's jeans were worn out and he carried an old leather rucksack. Sticking out the top of his pack was a fishing pole. He carried a guitar case in one hand and a leash in the other, followed by a black pit-bull dog. Passing the window, he noticed us staring, nodded and smiled.

"Poor fucker," my friend remarked, "things could be worse, we could be like him. Homeless!"

"He looks happy to me," I offered. "You see his smile?

When was the last time you smiled and meant it?"

As he walked away, I was struck with the idea that his life had more value, happiness and fulfillment than mine.

I suspected he felt sorry for us. There we sat, in ill-fitting suits and ties, worry and disdain furrowing our brow, anxiety and fear of failure our constant companion. Who would want to live like us?

Moonlight fills the freight car as it snakes along the winding terrain, making my shadow dance and contort. I am young and wild again. The summer night is filled with passion and ideas.

I wonder what Dave Thomson and my best friend, Mick Tripp, are doing now. Mick and I clocked up 25,000 miles riding the rails and hitchhiking in the early seventies. In 1974 we climbed aboard a westbound freight train at Roper Yard in May – the same train I'm riding now - and didn't climb off until November. We worked back and forth across America and Canada, meeting hundreds of people just like us, all searching for Amerika and lusting for adventure. We worked for a traveling carnival as set-up and breakdown laborers as it made stops at bucolic farming towns along the Mississippi River. I'll always remember the power of the river at night and the moonlight illuminating the cornfields. We ended up living with a group of Rosicrucians on a dairy farm in Minnesota. We milked cows by hand twice a day.

Dave Thomson a.k.a. Montana Dave, a.k.a. Minnesota Dave a.k.a. The Kid, rode the rails, too. He is the reason I'm here now. He is out here somewhere and I'm going to find him. As an investigative journalist I've learned to follow every lead to its end. The job is not finished until you do. David Thomson's mysterious disappearance haunts me, and now I have set aside my conventional life to find him.

Dave, Mick and I rode the rails at the same time. It could be that Mick and I ran into him somewhere out here. Unfortunately, I never knew the names of my most of my riding companions or if I did, they slipped unnoticed out the back door of my memory as new names and memories pushed in the front door. Still, I'm convinced there is a connection between Dave and myself; something tells me I knew him and that I am the one who will solve his vexing puzzle and find him.

It could be that Dave, Mick and I shared a joint at one of the many rail camps, or a bottle of rotgut wine in the tall fragrant grass along some Mississippi River byway. Mick and I were once chased off the Reno freight yard by the railroad bulls in the middle of the night, along with twenty other people packed on several open westbound freight cars. We all ended up on the I-80 westbound on-ramp hitchhiking. Dave could have been there that night.

I remember a tall, handsome young man who seemed keen to talk, and something clicked between us. We might have shared the indignity of being treated like modern day Mexican workers by the Sparks police that night.

Riding across the plains of Manitoba our train stopped at a forgotten siding in the middle of endless farm fields. The rail crew cut away a line of covered hoppers and empties, then disappeared, stranding maybe ten of us in the middle of a million square miles of nothing. Dave could have been there.

We spent an entire day backtracking along the rails to a two-lane highway and small farming community that sat on a hilltop, surrounded by fields sloping away like rice paddies. A towering blue mountain range climbed skyward to the north, its peaks beckoning and snow covered. In the middle ground, rolling hills washed against the mountains and were covered with deep pine forests. We gazed at the mysterious mountains in hungered silence. We were tired to the core, strangers one and all, but the sight of nature's magnificence astounded us. A tall thin man announced the distant shining mountains held some source of longing for him and he bid us farewell and disappeared over a hill.

I think it was Dave.

The desire to get back on the road, to live life in a different way is strong in some people. There are those among us who believe they can map out a life that is in some way unmediated by existing social restrictions and responsibilities. The writer and philosopher, Robert Pirsig, might call it a dynamic pattern of quality. It is that pre-intellectual movement toward the unknown, like riding the wave of new experience, not knowing what will happen next and being exhilarated by it. We have all experienced this feeling. It is the feeling of *truly* being alive. Yet most of us live sedentary lives and try to swallow back our longings so our safe, pathetic and stagnant existence can continue.

I'm convinced that people like David Thomson who disappear over the edge are hard-wired to do it. It may be the result of generations or eons of wandering, like the Bedouins of the Mideast or the tribesmen of northern Asia or the Indians of North America. At any given time, tens of thousands of people – some our friends and family – are part of this undercurrent of mobility.

Sometime during the night, I retrieve a stocking cap and some sweat pants. Summer nights in an open freight car are cold. I'm not sure when I fell asleep, but every time the train slowed or stopped I was awakened and could see lights of Nevada towns. In Battle Mountain, we changed crews and a railroad worker shined a flashlight into the car. I sat up on one elbow to see what was going on but by the time I did, he had moved on and I heard footsteps moving away. My riding companion hadn't stirred since climbing on board, except now he was mostly squeezed inside the sleeping bag.

As the new day revealed Sparks, I jumped from the car as it slowed into the rail yard. I knew better than to trespass railroad property. In years gone by, railroad workers didn't mind people hitching rides, but those days are gone. In the late 1980s, a new breed of outlaw rider changed all that and a series of murders stretching across the country, but mainly in the northwest corridor, created fear and anxiety among riders. Even today, more than one hundred murders occur on the rails every year.

My first stop on this search for Dave will be at an old hobo camp at the opposite side of the Sparks rail yard. It sits in a ravine under an old wood and steel trestle. The camp is known as a safe haven for riders associated with the FTRA, the Freight Train Riders of America.

A few blocks away from the yard I stop for breakfast at Ruby's Diner, an old greasy spoon in the low rent section of town. Taking a booth in the front window I start to order coffee, eggs and hash browns, but the waitress turned and walked away before I finish. The manager appears and asks if I have money to pay for the food. I retrieve a Visa card from the hidden pocket inside my waistband.

"You don't have cash?" he asked.

"You don't take credit?"

He turned the card over and over in his hand.

"Got a picture ID?"

"For coffee and eggs?"

He stood there unmoved.

I produced a driver's license from the same pocket.

"Sorry," he apologized, returning the card, "we get stiffed a lot. I thought you were one of the 'bos from the rail yard."

"I am," I answered, smiling. "Just rode in from Salt Lake. Beats flying any day."

Later at the hobo camp, every square inch of cement, wood or metal on the underside of the trestle was tagged with graffiti. Banksy had indeed been here. Large flaming red insignia's reading FTRA with lightning bolts or swastikas underneath were prominent. It was the Freight Train Riders Association emblem and this was its turf. There were many other tags too, mostly gang banger messages, one painted atop another. It would take all afternoon to search for any sign of Dave.

If anyone knew Dave Thomson or where he might be, it would be FTRA. There is an off-chance Dave is one of them. The FTRA is a shadowy group that some believe really doesn't exist and is nothing more than an urban legend, but those in law enforcement and those who ride the rails know they are out there. Authorities estimate more than a thousand members are riding the rails at any given time. They are losers and loners, forgotten men and women, veterans from Vietnam or Desert Storm - people who no longer have a country. They went off to war and never came home. The only place they fit in is out here where no one can get at them or tell them what to do. The only family they have is each other.

Sitting around a smoldering, half-dead campfire are Chipper, Dude Ranch and Weasel, a scarecrow-thin meth addict with the letters FTRA tattooed across the knuckles of his left hand. They are summer regulars who travel the High Line.

"Got a smoke?" Weasel inquires as I walk up.

"Wish I did," I reply, slapping an imaginary shirt pocket.

Weasel pulls out a wooden kitchen match and snaps it once with his thumbnail, sending up a flare of light. With his other hand, he theatrically pulls a flattened Marlboro from behind his ear and puts it to his lips.

"It's okay, man," he says, making the derm dance between his lips. "Got one already."

Weasel is bent over and bald, probably in his early forties, but he looks much older. He is terminally thin and toothless. I learn later that Weasel considers himself a ladies' man. He works his jaw muscles, and takes long contemplative drags from his cigarette while sizing me up. He is the gatekeeper of this camp - no one enters without his once over.

"Have a seat, man," he finally offers. "Where you comin' from?"

"Rode outta Roper yesterday on the old Rio Grande."

"You shittin' me?" he says, narrowing his eyes and smiling. "Shit Lake Salty! Fuckin' U-P (Union Pacific Railroad) owns that line now. Ain't too happy about that. I avoid Utah at all cost. Mormon zombies - like the walking dead."

"Had to get out..." I respond, "got one of the only open cars."

"Cock suckers! Lockin' up all the empties now. I'm going to burn 'em down!"

Chipper is the fire tender and collects the un-burned

ends of wood around the fire's perimeter and pushes them into the pit.

"Where you headin'?" he asks. Chipper reminds me of the cowardly lion in The Wizard of Oz. His lion's head mane and full beard frames a round, red and friendly face.

"Don't know," I answer, taking a seat on an old log. "Trying to catch up to a friend. Thought he might be around here. Might do the Feather River over to Orville or Sacto. Maybe hitch into Frisco. Got friends there."

"Winter over the Sierra?" Chipper asks, raising his bushy eyebrows, shaking his head and eyeing my pack, "Better have some long johns in there."

"Not to worry, I'm tankin' up on antifreeze," I answer, pulling my pack into the dirt and opening it so everyone can see the only thing inside is a bunch of clothes and an unopened five-liter box of pink Chablis.

"Compliments of Safeway," I announce, pulling the box out. "They forgot to charge me. Imagine that!"

Weasel snickers and nods his approval.

"Care for a bite?" I ask, handing Chipper the box.

"Fuckin-A," he sings.

A train's horn sounds and everyone stops and turns to acknowledge a departing train.

"Catchin' out," Dude Ranch announces, slapping his

hands down onto his knees and standing up. "That'll be my ride."

Dude grabs the box of wine, tips his head back and drains off mouthfuls, as the overflow fills his grizzled beard and runs down his neck. His hair and beard are long, matted and wild.

"I'm comin' in a day or two," Weasel shoots a look his way, "Save some of that pussy for me."

"You snooze, you lose," Dude laughs and leans forward, cutting loose with a huge belch in Weasel's face. "That's all I'm saving for you." He turns and climbs the hill behind the camp and disappears.

No sooner had Dude departed than Ellen arrives. She appears sick, shaky and emaciated. Her legs are nothing more than two spindly sticks with knots where her knees belong. Standing on the pathway she is wearing an old stained white tank top with shorts and calls out for "Kenny."

Weasel turns, shakes his head and bellows, "You're not supposed to come down here!"

"Please…"

"Police following you?"

"No… please."

Ellen keeps her arms folded against her concave chest.

She pulls on a cigarette and smokes goes in, but nothing comes out. Ellen is one of the walking dead and these citizens occupy every town and city in America. We see them, yet they somehow remain invisible to us. Her eyes are sunken and dart back and forth. Her face is skeletal and as she puffs on her cigarette, she shifts her weight from foot to foot. I think she might cry.

"Please!" she pleads.

Weasel takes Ellen by the elbow, turns her around and walks her back up the trail and out of sight.

Chipper is watching me.

"HIV," he says, making eye contact.

"Right," I look down.

"He pimps her out for smokes and meth."

"Someone pays for that?"

Silence.

"She was a singer."

"In a band?"

"Yeah, in England. Even well known."

A few minutes pass and Weasel a.k.a. Kenny reappears walking with a bouncy pimp roll.

"Crank?" he announces, working his jaw and gulping air. "Five bucks."

"Fuck no!" I reply, "I'm too old for that shit. I'd have

THE CAPITAL OF PARADISE: A MEMOIR

a coronary."

"Never too old, man," he says, pulling a new pack of Marlboro's from his pocket and smacking it hard against the knuckles of the back of his other hand; a fresh bloody knot stands out along a blue vein on the inside of his arm.

"I'll take one," Chipper pipes up.

"What?"

"A smoke."

Weasel hesitates.

"You owe me."

"Right. Right."

A few minutes later, my giant boxcar companion arrives. His sleeping bag is tied around his waist and one hand cups his ear, half coagulated blood oozing through his fingers.

With a sad look, he announces, "Phlear."

"What?"

"Phlear!"

"Ear?"

"Phlear!"

"Okay," I answer.

Silence.

"Get in a fight?"

He ignores my question and sits next to me on the old

tree trunk, holding his left hand to his ear.

Weasel is speechless and dwarfed by the giant. He steps back, narrows his eyes, and inhales deeply on his cigarette.

This man is not just large but gigantic, perhaps seven-feet-tall and four hundred pounds. I feel small and uncomfortable next to him.

Chipper kicks back in his broken down white plastic chair and gives me the dead eye, as if to ask what was going down.

"We shared the ride from Roper," I offer, shrugging. "Don't know 'im. Doesn't speak English."

Weasel is uneasy and stands away, arms crossed.

Turning to the giant, I enquire, "English?"

He shrugs his shoulders and shakes his head from side to side.

"English?" I repeat.

He ignores me and his attention drifts away into the fire's embers.

For a while we sit quietly, gazing into the fire, passing the box of wine and lost in thought. Firelight dances off the old wood and metal trestle as the night deepens. The sound of an occasional dog barking or a crew switching cars filters down to the dry riverbed camp.

I feel close to Dave Thomson here, as if he had just left a few minutes ago. This is the very hobo camp that David Thomson wrote about in the first scene of his book, *The Solar Kid*. It isn't exactly as he describes it, except for the old trestle, but it *is* this very camp.

Because Thomson wrote about this place, I decided to start my search here. Like many who visit these invisible places, Dave was part warrior and part lost soul. He was a social revolutionary who hated what America had come to represent. I suspect he felt helpless to really change anything so he dropped out – disappearing into the parallel world of the underground.

After his first book, *In The Shining Mountains*, published by Alfred Knopf in 1979 became a great success, he wrote, *The Solar Kid*, but refused to send it to his agent in New York as his contract stipulated. He decided instead to give it to his mother for safe keeping, telling her it would be worth something one day. The last time anyone saw Dave he was standing on the roadside hitchhiking west out of town. His brother later found a cryptic note in the glove box of Dave's VW bug. It thanked everyone for the love gifted him, but said he failed and didn't deserve another chance. He announced he was never coming back.

Sometime after the last rays of dusk disappeared, the

THE CAPITAL OF PARADISE: A MEMOIR

three seasoned ghost riders I'd seen in Roper yard arrived. They were a family, Gene, known as Wild Bill, and his sons, Cody and Jesse.

Weasel and Chipper greeted Wild Bill warmly; they were obviously comrades. Wild Bill proudly introduced his sons and said they were making their way up to the High Line. I sensed they were running from something. Bill was on edge and positioned himself so he could see anyone entering camp.

After introductions, everyone's attention turns to the giant who is oblivious to the new arrivals. He gazes into the fire and does not acknowledge the newcomers.

Weasel offers the box of wine to them.

"Christ Almighty," Wild Bill says, reading the label and wiping his mouth with the back of his hand. "You gotta be shittin' me... pink fuckin' Chablis!"

"A gift from Safeway," Weasel remarks, taking credit for the heist.

"If I drink this shit will I turn into a fucking pussy?" he barked and paused for effect, "like my man Chipman over here?"

Cody and Jesse wince with embarrassment.

Chipper smiles widely, showing his bad teeth, "Just in case, you better keep your butt hole puckered tight."

Rocking back and forth, I hold my breath waiting to see how the wild one responds.

"Been wonderin' about you for a long time, pretty boy." Bill says, shooting a glance at Chipper. "Only thing getting near my asshole is turds, TP and hemorrhoids!"

Cody and Jesse are now having the time of their lives; slapping their knees, laughing loudly and pushing each other back and forth. Bill passes the box to Cody.

Wild Bill had been a biker and still considered himself one. He laments, "Only now, I ain't got a bike."

He explains, "Got in a god-damn fight in Dallas over some stupid bitch and ended up stabbing her brother. Dumb bastard!

"It was me or him, kill or be killed! Didn't want to stick 'em but I had to," Bill paces back and forth. "Good goddamn thing I didn't hit 'em in an artery. I'd still be in that goddamned jail. Had 'ta put my wheels up – collateral." He pauses as if hurt, "Bailed out, twenty-five-thousand!"

Cody and Jesse knew the story, but were still inconsolable. There they sat, two forty-year-old men, hunched over, hands in their laps, glum expressions on their faces, staring into the fire. We all sat quietly for a long time.

"Had to get out of Dodge," Bill finally announces disgusted. "Before the prick died. Wasn't my fault! Just defending myself."

Wild Bill was showing his boys the rail circuit that starts in Texas on the Southern Corridor; traveling west on the CSX to the west coast, then back across the High Line from Seattle to Minneapolis. The plan changed after they spotted railroad bulls and police in Albuquerque. They jumped a train heading north and ended up in Denver. From there, they rode the Rockies on the old Rio Grande line outside of Five Points.

"In Querque," he continues, "we ran into Colton and Jack down by the river. Jack ain't doing well. He took a 30-foot fall off a roof working for a contractor down in Tempe. Fucked up his back big-time. Rowdy is still livin' under a freeway overpass. Shit, that ain't no way to live! Got to be near sixty-five. Says he needs to stay put, to get his social security check."

"Fuck that social security shit," Weasel pipes up.

"After Seattle," Wild Bill goes on, "we're headin' up north to Montana Dave's old camp. I hear Jerry and Leon been livin' there since Vegas."

"Montana Dave?" I ask.

"Know him?"

"Don't know," I answer. "I'm trying to catch up to an old traveling buddy, Dave Thomson. We go back to Nam.

Some call him Montana Dave. Lived up in the woods near Glacier. Goes by Minnesota Dave, Solar Dave and The Kid."

"Ain't the same Dave," Chipper says, stroking his beard and shaking his head. "Unless he is dead. How long since you seen him?"

"Been a few years now. I got to worrying, so here I am."

"Could be the same Dave, then." Chipper admits. "Never heard of Solar Dave."

"Dead?" I ask.

"Somebody pushed Dave in front 'a line of moving cars outside the Spokane rail yard," Weasel adds. "Cut him right in half - up the middle."

"If I find out who did it," Bill says, neck muscles bulging and voice rising with each word. "I'll take the mother fucker apart."

"Me too." Weasel hisses.

"Ain't been the same without Dave… or the rest…" Chipper says sadly. "People disappearing right and left. Dying off, I guess. Nobody left."

"Those were the days, weren't they?" Bill reflects, looking at his boys. "Those days are long gone. It used to be a brotherhood. Everyone got along - no beefs or hostilities… no fucking illegal aliens."

Turning to Bill, Chipper asks, "Wasn't Montana Dave from Minnesota?"

"Hell, I don't know. Could have been. Sounds good to me," Bill shakes his head and gets back to his story. "Now days, we get all the fucking college pricks riding the rails for kicks. They think it's some fucking Disneyland mother-fucker. Threw two of them off a boxcar a year or so back." He smiles widely, eyes glistening. "Bet they weren't too happy about that. Especially since we were on going forty miles an hour."

Everyone except for the giant smiles and laughs.

"All we got left of Dave now is his signature over there," Weasel points to a slab of concrete under the trestle. "Put it there himself."

"Where?" I ask.

"Up in the middle," Chipper says, pointing. "See the letters in red paint?"

I move closer before spotting them. There they were: M.D.T.

"There! Right?"

I couldn't believe my good luck. My hunch about Dave Thomson might play out.

"What's the T stand for?" I ask, excited.

"Don't know," Chipper answers.

"Hell if I know," Weasel adds.

"The Dave I'm looking for is Dave Thomson."

"I'll be damned," Weasel says, shaking his head, "Never knew Dave's last name. Could be him."

CHAPTER THIRTEEN

DANCING ON THE HEAD OF SERPENTS

Dying *is* big businesses in sunny Scottsdale where tens of thousands of Raisins – tanned, wrinkled and affluent Boomers – live out their golden years. Everything a person needs to live and die well – sun, warmth, great food, entertainment – are close at hand. World-class medical centers like the Mayo Clinic dot the landscape and an army of doctors and oncologists practice here. Nearly everyone over the age of sixty-five qualifies for a medical marijuana card and the high-end cannabis options are endless. The local joke in Scottsdale is to be on the lookout for Raisins smoking Lunar Nougats and racing their convertible BMWs and Corvettes up the Carefree Highway for brunch in tony Cave Creek.

Today is my first day of chemotherapy and the Copperwood Cancer Center foyer is packed with dying people. The spacious and sunny atrium reminds me of a fashionable beauty salon and is decorated with fresh flowers and stylish leather chairs. Yet something is amiss here – smiling faces. A sun-drenched silence denotes the deep dread and sadness.

Terrified patients suffocate on craven fear while waiting for their name to be called. They will soon disappear behind the curtain into the magical chemo room where toxic and poisonous chemicals will be pumped into their veins by attentive nurses in a misguided effort to give them a few extra low-quality days at the end of life.

I imagine a future America where entrepreneurs combine the cancer chemo center with a one-stop, self-indulgent shopping experience for psychological counselors, opioids, hospital bed rental equipment, home nursing and hospice care and colorful catalogs showcasing mausoleums, silk and fur lined coffins, crypts, plots and cremation services all at the same time.

Waiting my turn I notice few patients interact or even acknowledge their fellow travelers. Each is sequestered inside his or her own private anguished hell. Beautiful and desperate older couples sit quietly holding hands; time is short and the heartache is impossible to hide. One smartly dressed bald woman sits with her head down looking into her hands. She turns them over and over while muttering and crying softly to herself. I'm wearing my smart Dolce and Gabbana shades and no one knows I'm watching. Working men and women are here, too. They look uncomfortable slouching and shifting from bun to bun and avoiding their anxiety by blankly staring into the smartphone digital morass. I imagine they are antsy to escape, to shrug off this masquerade and return to their jobs, families and mortgage payments. There are young people here, too. They are the most tragic and stand out like frightened owlets with round eyes blinking. They offer a sweet naiveté so missing without them.

This incongruous medical scene reminds me of my first introduction to civil society and mass medicine during the mid 1950s with the polio epidemic. Early one cold wintery December morning the Taylor family arrived at the Murray City courthouse where hundreds of townsfolk were already lined up to get the first in a series of three polio shots. There were good morning greetings, smiles and the enthusiasm of big unit America, but even as a five-year-old I could tell this was a serious life and death business. I remember waiting nearly two hours in the cold before the line snaked indoors and down a long hallway into a room where nurses busily swabbed arms, gave painful shots and placed Band-Aids on our bare shoulders. Much has changed since those days. We were a cohesive group back then, the American people, but today we are merely consumers being monetized by a profit driven capitalist health care enterprise.

When my name is called I feel it's a mistake and make a half-bleating noise like a frightened slaughterhouse lamb. Still, I stand ramrod straight in a dignified manner and follow the nurse through the shroud into the inner sanctum where I meet my oncologist, Dr. Bakia. I learn later that Bakia is a Svengali of sorts, the only person I've ever met who can enter and exit a room at the same time. In response to his fast moves, I leap in front of the doorway and block his retreat when I need his undivided attention. I'm paying for this, right? In rapid fire perfect English he tells me how busy he is, that my blood work looks good, and then pushes past me to leave. As if an afterthought, he half-turns and over his shoulder asks if I have questions. Before I can respond he disappears into a nearby examination room. I should feel fortunate to have him, but he needs me more than I need him. I am one of the nearly dead and he needs to keep me alive so he can make the monthly payments on his beautiful new Mercedes AMG sitting out in the parking lot.

The chemo room is all business. The rectangular space

is filled with ivory leather reclining chairs sitting in a large semi-circle. Each chair has a small table on one side and an IV stand on the other. I sit next to a short round woman in her sixties who is hairless and has an inflatable plastic helmet pulled down to her eyebrows and makes a soft hissing air compressor noise. This odd apparatus pumps cold air to the head when certain toxic chemicals are administered into the brain. At one end of the room is a nurse's station and the place is busy with perhaps ten nurses and aids helping deliver chemicals by IV drip to two dozen patients.

On the drive home I feel dizzy and nauseous. A metallic taste coats my mouth. My lips and mouth are so dry I gulp down an entire bottle of cold water, but the dryness does not dissipate. Suddenly, I start to heave and pull the car to the edge of the road where I barely get the door open before I throw up repeatedly until there is nothing left. I will dry heave on and off for hours. My head swims and my brain feels like the electrical impulses carrying my thoughts are disrupted or disconnected. Desperate, I attempt to lie down across the front seat but the console makes that impossible. It becomes apparent I need to sit up and keep my head above my body. I feel it is imperative for my survival. If I lay down I will pass out or worse.

I am overcome with nausea and sit with my legs outside the car and I cradle my scrambled head in my hands. I writhe and dry heave again and for the next while I sit unmoving, feeling any movement will start the spinning and nausea again. By the time I get home I am being eaten alive from the inside out. I can't breathe and rush outside into the 109-degree heat. I still can't breathe, but now I'm being incinerated from the inside out and the outside in.

For the next number of days – I'm not sure how many – I'm bedridden and on a rotisserie, spinning round and round, unable to find relief from the unrelenting pain, nausea and internal burning. Before leaving the chemo center, a nurse attached an on-body injector, set to automatically release a potent chemical a day later, one that attacks the bones to stimulate the production of white blood cells needed to fight infection. For the first time ever, I feel every bone in my skeleton throbbing and aching like an excruciating abscessed tooth.

The pained look on Lana's face is frightening. She desperately wants to help and I hear her crying in the bathroom when she thinks I can't hear. She would do anything to give me relief and feels somehow responsible for pushing the chemo option. We discussed chemotherapy many times and while we did not know if it would help or be a problem unto itself, we both acknowledged that no chemo would leave me with no options and little time left. Advanced scans show I have bone cancer tumors on my hips, left femur, ribs and spinal column. One large tumor sits at the base of my spinal column and another at the very top. Bone cancer tumors dissolve healthy bone causing it to break or collapse. A failure of any bones in the spinal column would be extremely painful and would lead to severe disability.

After ten or so days the bone pain dissipates somewhat and I am left with a droning hum ringing endlessly in my skull. The vibration causes a numbingly debilitating cognitive deficit. I feel my head is underwater and all sounds are muted and distorted. Breathing is a chore and I constantly feel as if I'm suffocating. My eyes refuse to focus so reading or watching television is out. Every time I leave the bed I fall over and must crawl to the bathroom. My urine is bright cooper colored and constipation creates crushing pressure on my abdominal cavity. My kidneys ache and I experience a constant painful roiling. Within days, I develop painful and bloody sores in my mouth, nose, lips and sinuses.

To stave off this onslaught I curl into a fetal position and retreat deep inside myself. I sing my favorite songs and attempt to focus on better times and memories. I search for an acknowledgment that life is more than my current insufferable situation. My thoughts drift far afield and I find some solace in memories of the good old days.

CHAPTER FOURTEEN

RIO VERDE

Pain Drug Hypnosis

Just got off the phone with the Church of Scientologist's lead attorney and church leader David Miscavige's best friend Bill Walsh, a man considered a bona fide hero by most Scientologists. Walsh is the go-to guy for high profile legal crises. He and Miscavige are tight and he drops the big guy's name "Dave" whenever possible. Walsh was the lead attorney for the church in its historic fight with the IRS to obtain not-for-profit status in the late 1990s.

Bill wants to know how the book is going. He is interested in the chapter I'm working on right now, the battle between the church, the American Psychiatric Association and government intelligence agencies (CIA and FBI) during the 1950s and 1960s. Someone must have told him about my repeated requests for information.

Bill is an affable guy who knows how to connect with

people on a personal level.

"Bill, for the life of me," I tell him, "I can't get anyone to supply me with the Hubbard quotes (the quotes proving Hubbard repeatedly spoke up against the secret mind control operations run by U.S. intelligence services and American Medical Association). The PR department and Richard in history profess to know about them, but no one has produced them. Everyone passes me off to someone else. I'm wondering if they even exist."

"I'll see what I can find and get back to you."

CREATION STORIES

With these three words, "In the beginning," Christianity's story of creation begins.

Most religions in the Western tradition have creation stories. These stories are really tapestries of hundreds of individual stories stitched together to form a history and belief system. In the case of Christianity, these stories are two thousand years old and were passed down from one person to the next until the advent of transcription. Some stories are fairly ludicrous, but so much time has elapsed they can't be rebutted or verified so they fall into the realm of faith and belief.

When a story is told again and again over an extended

period it works its way into the lexicon of fact and becomes part of a history. Most religions – Buddhism, Judaism, Christianity, Islam and Native American beliefs – have legend of creation stories telling what they believe and how it came into being. These creation stories become enshrined in the foundational structure of the organization and are retold in perpetuity. Many religions have ancient origins and the creation stories defy fact checking efforts because they occurred hundreds or thousands of years earlier. But this is not the case with the Church of Scientology.

In the case of a new religion like Scientology, its creation story is just 60 years old and in some respects is still being written.

One aspect of Scientology history and part of its creation story has confounded me. It is a small but important and essential element I'm uncomfortable including in this book without verifiable evidence and secondary substantiation. I have been given carte-blanche access to all church libraries and archives, as well as Hubbard speeches and I have logged months of intensive research. As yet I have been unable to actually locate the quotes or corresponding evidence of its existence.

It relates to L. Ron Hubbard leading the effort to unmask and expose the CIA, U.S. military and American Psychiatric Association for its unconscionable, inhumane and illegal mind control experiments on unwitting American citizens from the early 1950s to the 1970s. Church history and its contemporary public relations material has it that Hubbard was an outspoken critic about this egregious situation and railed against it many times in speeches, workshops and seminars.

There is no dispute that Hubbard was the first American to bring this situation to the public's attention. But so far I have seen little evidence that he led an ongoing effort to expose the CIA or psychiatry and their involvement.

This might seem inconsequential, but the church claims that as a result of Hubbard's ongoing public denunciations the church was subsequently attacked and investigated by the FBI, IRS and media at the behest of military intelligence and the medical community. So this minor issue takes on a much greater and more significant role.

Here is what I know and can substantiate:

In 1950 after *Dianetics: The Modern Science of Mental Health* was published people from across the country sought out Hubbard and asked for his help. Many people had strikingly similar stories of mysterious bouts of sleeplessness, periods of time they could not account for, unexplained bruises, sores and broken teeth, symptoms of amnesia and strange dreams of medical treatments they could not recall. Many had been patients at leading universities or elite medical centers. Even more came from mental hospitals, military prisons or psychiatric wards.

With each new case, Hubbard's suspicions grew. Using techniques developed for Dianetics and written about in his book, Hubbard identified ways to bring these perplexing symptoms to the surface. He pieced together that these individuals had been guinea pigs in a vast conspiracy to develop and perfect mind control techniques. These test participants were hypnotized and post hypnotic suggestions were implanted so they had no memory of what happened afterwards.

In his 1951 follow-up book, *Science of Survival: Simplified, Faster Dianetic Techniques*, Hubbard unmasked the government and psychiatry's secret mind control experiments. He delivered a broadside and announced what he discovered. He wrote, *"There is another form of hypnotism which falls between the surgical operation and straight hypnotism without physical pain. This form of hypnotism has been a carefully guarded secret of certain military and intelligence organizations. It is a vicious war weapon and may be of considerably more use in conquering a society than the atom bomb. This is no exaggeration. The extensiveness of the*

use of this form of hypnotism in espionage work is so wide
today that it is long past the time when people should have
become alarmed about it. It required Dianetics processing to
uncover pain-drug-hypnosis. Otherwise, pain-drug-hypno-
sis was out of sight, unsuspected, and unknown."

At the time of this passage, Mr. Hubbard knew of the
intelligence community's work, but it is doubtful he knew
the actual extent or colossal size and scope of these out-of-
control projects. There is no doubt however, that his state-
ments did not go unnoticed by both US intelligence and
the psychiatric community.

In the intervening years, the FBI and IRS leveled one
allegation after another of wrongdoing against the church
and Hubbard. Along with the American Medical Association and the American Psychiatric Association, it appears
that a well-planned and organized attack was made against
Scientology and Hubbard.

Scientologists maintain this quote and his frequent
calling attention to these mind control experiments brought
on the investigations. It all makes good sense, but I can
only find two other minor references of Hubbard speaking out about this subject. At this point, I'm beginning to
believe that years ago one exaggeration led to another and
now this inaccurate piece of Scientology's history i.e., that

Hubbard spoke out frequently and led the movement to expose it, has solidified and become part of the church's creation story. In my view, without supporting evidence, the claim that Hubbard led a vocal opposition should not be included in this definitive account of church history.

Chapter Fifteen

Rio Verde

There are days I think of my mother and what she went through at the end of her life. I wonder about what she must have been thinking. There was nothing I could do – nothing anyone could do – except take care of her and this haunts me. I remember as a boy how every once in a while she would break down and cry for no apparent reason. When I asked about it, she'd shake her head and say, 'Oh Mark, I guess I'm just thinking about my mum and how I miss her.'

I see my mother standing in the backyard gardens of random houses as I pass along the highway. She is in the tomato patch, wearing a summer dress and waving up at me. I see her silhouette lying along distant mountain ranges and in wisps of evening skies. I smell her fragrance in every department store and I hear her laughter sailing across time back to me. She knows all the old songs and dance movie tunes. I imagine us at the Taylor homestead sipping tea from her mother's English teacups, then doing a few step-ball-changes on the hard kitchen floor. We are together and everything is different, but gratefully, the same.

SALT LAKE CITY, UTAH
SEPTEMBER 11, 1995
AFTER MIDNIGHT

Somewhere in the unattached darkness a midnight freight train blasts its whistle and the mournful song carries across the valley and into the living room where my mother lies in her hospital-style bed. Although June B. Taylor is dying of brain cancer and has fallen into a coma, she begins to writhe gently, to flail her arms and legs, to move her head from side to side as if she heard the train's whistle. My sister Nancy and I are watching from either side of the bed.

"I wonder if Daddy has come for her?" Nancy asks.

"I hope so," I answer.

You see, my father had been a railroad man. He was a real railroad man; tough, straightforward and responsible. My sister Nancy called him Daddy. I called him Pop. Pop died several years earlier but he had always been there for his sweetheart when she needed him. Could it be that our father has transcended death to fly back on the train's whistle; reassure her of his presence, and tell her it was time to join him?

It all started just eleven short weeks ago. In that time our family felt the incomprehensible pain of tragedy so deeply and all encompassing, it was impossible to plumb the depth of it. We traveled roads of desperation, of dashed hopes, of devastating realities, of angry conflict and profound sorrows. It was too real, but unreal at the same time. Our mother had gone from being a beautiful, healthy, classy, vivacious and engaging woman to a lifeless form lying in a coma, just a few breaths away from eternity. How could this have happened?

It all began on the warm summer morning of June 23, 1995, when at age 71, she just stopped in her tracks – like a terracotta soldier frozen mid-stride. She made a cup of coffee, placed it on the dining room table and was about to sit down when she was disconnected.

I was in my downstairs office working on a new book and came up for coffee and saw her standing next to her chair. A half hour later when I returned, she was still standing in the exact place and in the same pose. "What's going on, Mother?"

No response.

"Why are you standing there?"

Still, no answer.

"Are you okay?"

Nothing.

"Mother! What's going on?" I ask frantically.

Nothing.

I look into her eyes. She was gazing down at the table and was smiling slightly. I shook her arm and tried to get her to respond.

Nothing.

I call 911 and my older sister, Carol.

One day later when the neurosurgeon came to mother's room with the MRI scans and told us of the diagnosis I felt as if I might faint. I had a sense of disbelief. We all did.

Mother had a stage four primary brain tumor called a glioblastoma. A primary brain cancer means the tumor had its origin in the brain and glioblastoma is the fastest growing, most deadly type of brain tumor. The diagnosis is always terminal. A neurosurgeon told me privately, "I've treated hundreds of glio patients over the past ten years and not one survived."

Mother's tumor was the size of a small egg and located in the brain's left temporal lobe, what the neurosurgeon called, "The center of human eloquence; the place where emotion, intellect and creativity interact to form personality." They couldn't say what caused it or how long it had been there, or more importantly, how fast it was growing. I found out later, they didn't know.

The doctor outlined two treatment plans. The first was to essentially do nothing. We would take our mother home, make her comfortable, give her love and wait. The doctor said if we did nothing, in his opinion, she had three or four months. The second plan was aggressive, he would biopsy the tumor to get more information, and then perform surgery to remove as much of the tumor as possible, followed by radiation and then chemotherapy. This might extend mother's life a few months or maybe even a year. But, this plan was not without great risks. Surgery could make her worse, she could be left disabled or even paralyzed.

When the doctor left, we were stunned and stood in silence. From her bed, mother smiled and asked, "What did he say? Am I going to be alright?"

"No, Mother," I told her, "you've got a tumor in your brain."

She smiled and asked, "Is it cancer?"

"Yes. It's called a glioblastoma."

"Oh," she said, "am I going to die?" She smiled as if embarrassed by the preposterous nature of the question.

Four days later we took her home. Because she had been prescribed steroids and other medications to reduce the swelling of the brain, her main symptom, and dysphasia – the inability to speak and to comprehend – had, to a degree, disappeared. Surprisingly, she had no pain. I found out later that brain tumors are painless; there are no nerve endings in the brain. We also learned that each brain tumor victim has a unique set of symptoms, based on variables such as the type of tumor (there are more than 100), whether it is benign or malignant, its size and location and especially, its rate of growth. If a tumor is growing slowly, symptoms may stay relatively the same, but if it grows quickly, symptoms change rapidly.

At first, mother was lucid and sometimes articulate, enough so to have one of us take her to the bank so she could get cash. She gave the money to us kids, to the grandkids, to friends she loved, and to almost anyone she saw. She put hundred dollar bills in her pockets and forgot about them; she stuffed them down between couch cushions. "What did I do with all that money?" she asked. "Did I spend it or did you take it?" We took her to the bank again and again.

For two weeks there was a strange foreboding calm. Mother rose early, made coffee and spent a few hours in her beloved flower beds. She hummed tunes from the 1940s as she walked along the beds. She enjoyed the beauty, the fragrances and the splendor of it all. The flower beds had always been more than her garden; they connected her to her own mother who had died many years earlier. Many of mother's flowers had come from her mother's garden.

As days passed, the dysphasia worsened. She was frustrated when she could not find the right words. She was desperate to communicate and quickly developed an Esperanto language of shorts, a combination of word roots, gestures and facial expressions. It was like playing charades and we had fun doing it. This worked well at first, but it became more difficult every day. She knew something was terribly wrong, but sometimes she could not entirely grasp it or its implications – or at least, that is how it appeared to us. One of the terrible things for us was wondering how much she comprehended. Was she at peace or terrified?

Throughout this period, her beautiful, loving personality survived. She was delightful and friendly and outgoing. She still spoke in a guileless and unpretentious way. To strangers, she might say, "Do you know what I have… what is happening to me… that I have… brain… it's alright, Dolly… don't be sad…I love you, too."

At night, she and I would watch TV until after midnight. It had been our routine before her illness. As usual, before going to bed we would embrace, but now we hugged as we never had before. It was an embrace of loving desperation. We languished in one another's arms – mother and son – son and mother – knowing that one day soon we would never embrace again.

Later, I would lay awake and worry. What was going to happen to us? What were we to do? The doctors had written her off. They seemed so tentative and wimpy. I felt as if I should not believe anything they said. My sisters accepted the diagnosis and wanted to do nothing, not to have anyone operate on mother; to spare her the pain of being less, when all options were terminal.

If they operated she would get a few months at best; and at what cost, being an invalid, a veritable vegetable? She would never have wanted that and we all knew it. But I, on the other hand, needed to fight the diagnosis, to find a way, if possible, out of this; a clinical study maybe, an experimental treatment, another doctor. I desperately want a silver bullet, a way things could return to normal, a way we all could go on for a little longer. She would have fought for me, gone hammer and tong with anyone to save me. In retrospect, I know it was selfish of me, but I loved her and could not face the idea of living without her.

I took her for a second opinion, then a third. I hung on every word, on every nuance, on every posture the neurosurgeon made. I found hope in consultations that contained no hope. A friend, a librarian at a famous medical center, researched brain tumors and printed out 500 pages that included 2,500 case and clinical studies. I poured over them night and day searching each page as if it might hold the secret to saving my mother. My sister Nancy once told a hospice worker, "If Mark could find a cure for mother by educating himself, she would be well again." Nancy was right. I know that now.

But there were real questions that needed to be answered. How fast was the tumor growing? When did it start and how old was it? Had it been there for a long time, dormant? Or, had it appeared quickly, growing out of control like... cancer? How had she developed it? What could have caused it? Why did it strike her? Was it genetic? Was it aspartame, whose brand name was NutraSweet? Mother had been a fan of NutraSweet. I decided that if it was NutraSweet and I could prove it, I would buy a handgun and assassinate the company's president.

Would she have three months, six months, a year, or

would she drop dead tomorrow? I wanted to get a biopsy of the tumor so we would have a better understanding of its heinous nature and how we might proceed. My sisters were against it.

We began to argue, to scream, to make preposterous allegations and accusations against each other. We traded hurtful insults as mother sat, smiling among us. The rancor was intense. We were divided by our views of the right way to protect her. We were trying to do the right thing, as surely she would have done for us. Yet we found ourselves on opposite sides of the fence, with them accepting the diagnosis and wanting to make mother comfortable. They would not have a surgeon mucking around in her head, risking or destroying the last bit of her. I wanted action; I wanted a clinical study, an experimental treatment, surgery. Anything! I went a little crazy.

In the final analysis, my sisters were right and I was wrong. I held out hope that just maybe her tumor was growing very slowly. Yet as days turned into weeks and her symptoms changed and became more difficult, I could not escape the reality of what was happening.

Every few days mother's symptoms were changing, getting worse. Her vocabulary went from thousands of words, to hundreds of words, to scores of words, to just a handful. But just when we were convinced she was truly gone, unable to string a group of words together to make a sentence, she returned to us for a minute or two. Suddenly, out of the mist she would arrive, "If I'm going to die, why operate?" she once asked. "I love you. I want you to be happy. Don't be sad about me. Don't fight. I want us all to get along now." Another time, "I'm going away to go be with Pop and mother." Then, just as unexpectedly as she had arrived, she was gone again.

One day in the sixth week, she sat at the dining room table and spent the entire morning writing me a letter. Her posture and demeanor told me it was important. She was having great difficulty. I will never know what her intention was, but I believe she was telling me she loved me and to go on with my life.

She watched as I opened and read it. There were no understandable sentences and she had repeated the same words over and over again. It made no sense. When I finished looking at it I turned to her and we embraced, "Thank you. I love you too, mother."

About this same time she took up sitting in an old chair that had been out in the garage. She had us move it into the living room, and then began eating and ultimately sleeping there.

One day I heard her out in the flower garden and watched from the kitchen window as she went from one plant to the next spraying the blossoms and foliage. She was upset and talking gibberish. I quickly went out to find her spraying her blossoms with Round Up, a strong weed killer.

"Damned bugs!" she said with tears in her eyes.

I took the can of herbicide from her and gave her a can of insecticide. "This will probably work better."

Several days later, her flowers were dying and she frantically led me out into the garden where she pointed at the dying blossoms. She looked at me, raised and dropped her shoulders as if to say, "What's wrong?"

At eight weeks she was getting progressively worse; she was unable to talk and there were changes in her personality. She emptied clean dishes from the dishwasher and dropped them one by one onto the floor where they broke and made an enormous racket. She didn't notice. She poured a cup of hot coffee down the front of her and seemed oblivious to it. She put her blouses on backwards, and wore the same clothes day after day. The Esperanto language of gestures, word roots and facial expressions was no longer working. She gave us dirty looks, as if to say, "Why are you doing this to me?"

Nearly gone was the woman that people had loved. Nearly gone was the sentimental fool who would laugh until she cried as she looked at old family photographs. Nearly gone was the generous and loving sweetheart, the devoted cheerleader who stood up for all in bad times. Nearly gone was the woman who loved me, and who believed in me as no one had ever done.

For a few days in the eighth or ninth week she became mean and angry. This was difficult because she had always been so tender and loving. The medications bloated her face and her eyes were distant and dull. Several times, in the middle of the night, I was awakened by a loud crashing sound. I bolted up the stairs in the darkness to find her lying unconscious in one of the rooms. I will never forget the sheer terror I felt then – it was a nightmare. These blackouts marked the beginning of the end.

When we took her for her scheduled MRI the doctor was amazed that she was still on her feet. The tumor that had been the size of a small egg was the size of a large navel orange. The doctor looked at mother sitting quietly there and said, "It's truly amazing that she's still conscious. Look for yourself." We crowded around and the dispassionate MRI told the story.

During week number eleven, my sisters loaded mother into a car and drove her to Wendover, Nevada to gamble and have fun. It had been one of mother's favorite getaways. Before her illness, she and her friends would take the Fun Bus to Wendover to play the slot machines. By all accounts she had a blast that day. But by the time she got home she could no longer walk, so I assisted her into the house. I helped her into the bathroom where she stood before the mirror and seeing that her head was drooping, she lifted her chin proudly and elegantly, she straightened her beautiful salt and pepper hair with her fingers, and tried to apply fresh lipstick. She pursed her lips to accept the rouge, but her hand betrayed her and spread it across her face.

When the hospital bed came into the house the next day, she knew the end was near. We helped her out of her old chair and into the bed and then she motioned to each of us to come closer. One by one, she hugged us tightly – for the longest time. The meaning was clear, it was our last goodbye. It was an embrace that would have to last an eternity.

Within a day she fell into a coma.

The truly difficult things in life don't sink in quickly, especially death. On September 11, 1995, after a long night of labored breathing and with the sound of a freight train's whistles moving her one last time – she departed this life in pursuit of our father and her beloved mother. It had been eleven weeks from start to finish.

CHAPTER SIXTEEN

SOMEWHERE ALONG THE MISSISSIPPI RIVER

JULY 1974

The heat of a late July afternoon is slipping away as sunset gives way to dusk. Mick and I have found a bluff above the river carpeted in tall wheat-like grass that rolls down to the river's edge. The power of the river and the blue strobe of the fireflies creates a halcyon moment – and to top it off, Steppenwolf's *Born to be Wild* floats in and out from somewhere across the river.

This is what I went searching for – the experiences of serendipity where I wake up in the morning and have no idea where I'll lay my head at night. There is magic along this road life and many of us who went searching for America discovered both wonder and a simplicity we neither expected nor knew to exist.

Mick fusses with his pack before pulling out a half bottle of tequila and without ceremony chugs down a big pull. He sits straight up like Jack Nicholson's character, George, in the movie Easy Rider. He thrusts one hand into his armpit while flapping his other arm up and down like a bird and yelping out in delight. "Burns all the way down," his face distorts and grimaces.

Handing the bottle over to me I take a slow pull. "If you don't have anything to eat," I say, exhaling, "tequila is a good substitute."

When it comes to spirits Mick doesn't have an off switch. This has led to serious consequences and will again. One reason he tagged along was to avoid jail time back home. Mick and I are opposites in many ways. When it comes to alcohol I'm only good for a shot or two; on this night it has a medicinal purpose, killing my hunger pangs and setting my mind ablaze.

Dusk turns the shade under some nearby oak trees black and the river diverts straight down my gullet filling me up with a deep sense of a *real* life playing out. A half-mile to the north, the far side of the Savanna-Sabula Bridge disappears into night and from our vantage point the town of Savanna directly across the river is awash with the colorful lights of a carnival at the river's edge. The neon spokes of a Ferris wheel stretch out like abstract arms turning over and over again across the glassy surface of the water to create a light show Billy Graham and the Fillmore West would envy.

On perfect nights like this I float above myself and think of all the amazing things we've seen and done. Mick and I have been on the road six months now, traveling coast to coast by rail and hitch hiking. We know most of the good freeway on and off ramps and the places to sneak onto the rail yards without being seen. We've fallen asleep outside of Denver in Rocky Mountain National Park and awakened on the Golden Gate Bridge. We traveled for weeks with Billy Goodwin, a middle-aged man dying of lung cancer who wanted to see all those places he'd missed because of the responsibility he felt working a high paying union job in Ohio. "You don't just leave a good job like that for no good reason," he told us then laughed at his miscalculation.

I often think about my first love Lana who I'd left behind years earlier and wondered what she might be doing at that exact moment. It's hard to stop the heart from going where love and longing takes it. Sometimes the hurt is so intense I can't breathe.

Untying my sleeping bag from my pack I roll it out atop the grass and stretch out along its length. It fills good to lie flat, let my back stretch out and decompress. Above the western horizon the crescent moon and Venus kiss gently and the faint light from the Milky Way appears directly above.

Mick is drunk and sloppy. He tells me again the story about how his father, Blaine, tried to kill him while the entire family water skied on a high Uinta mountain lake. "The fucker gunned it with me hanging on to the ski rope for all I was worth. He went straight for the rocks on the other side, making a hard turn at the last second and whiplashing me around and sending me straight into the boulders."

I pretend I'm not listening so he changes the subject. "God damned, I'm hungry!" he shouts out. "We haven't eaten for days. We need to find some food – some real cheese and bread and salami and wine. Remember the sourdough on Fisherman's wharf?"

"In the morning we'll go across the river and see if the carnival over there needs some help," I add, lazily.

For the next hour, I am hypnotized by the river, the lights and the static electricity of the night. I am one with myself and marvel at this *Be Here Now* moment.

The next morning we wake early and hike across the bridge to the Holbert Traveling Carnival where we find work as laborers. For the next few weeks we work one riverside town after another, setting up and breaking down the traveling show. In between we do whatever backbreaking work they set us to doing. We are happy to be working and we call each other Carney. Within a week we are driving the trucks and forklifts; setting up tents and booths and rides and fixing whatever has broken. After the show closes on Saturday we work all night tearing everything down and loading it on the trucks. The rides are old and dangerous and the games of chance are rigged and mostly dishonest. But in the small family farming towns we visit, the people ignore our shortcomings and see us as colorful gypsies and are happy we are there. It is as if our presence brings the world of the weird to their doorstep. They often tell us to hurry back next year.

We are paid cash daily and when we accumulate two hundred bucks we bid the Holbert's goodbye and hitchhike north into Minnesota where an old antiwar friend, Dewayne Morgan owns an organic dairy farm.

Dewayne is a marine veteran who spent two tours in Vietnam before leaving the military and starting the Utah chapter of the Vets Against the Viet Nam War in Salt Lake City. We forged a close friendship during those tumultuous times and stood shoulder to shoulder as brothers. When the war was winding down, Dewayne moved to northern Minnesota and bought a farm. I promised him Mick and I would come help at harvest time and we arrive just as the work got started.

About forty miles outside of Park Rapids an old 1950s light blue GMC truck pulls over and offers us a ride.

"Where you headed?" the scruffy, unshaven man with a John Deere hat asks.

"Park Rapids," I respond.

"Sure enough, climb in. Me too - that's where I'm headed."

Throwing our packs in the bed of the truck, we climb into the cab.

After some small talk, Roger asks us what is in Park Rapids.

"I've got a friend up there," I tell him. "He owns a farm and we are going up to help him out."

Roger leans forward and takes a hard look at us; his wizened face is awash with wrinkles. "You must be the two city boys Dewayne Morgan is waiting on to come help with harvest."

"You know Dewayne?" I ask.

"Oh yeah, sure." Roger speaks slowly, elongating each word and placing emphasis on the word's ending. "He borrows my wind rower and pays me back by doing some welding for me."

"Small world," Mick comments.

"Oh sure enough is, everyone knows everyone else in Park Rapids. I live over on Long Lake and Dewayne is off SR-71 a few miles west."

Roger tells us about his corn crop and the damned low price he'll get later this fall on his cranberries. "Damn hard making ends meet for family farmers these days. Farming is the only business where folks buy at retail and sell at wholesale."

The farms and fields surrounding Park Rapids are picturesque and Roger pulls over on Main Street in front of the Homer Hotel. He points to a telephone booth standing next to the front door.

"Got Dewayne's number?" he asks.

"Right here," I retrieve my slim black leather diary and contact book.

"He should be home about now," Roger goes on. "He had to have some work done on his tractor this morning, but should be back home about now."

We thank him and retrieve our gear from the bed of the truck.

"Sure, glad to help," he says and continues. "I was wondering if you city boys might help me bale some hay for an afternoon after you get settled in?"

"No problem. We can help," I respond. "I'll need to

talk to Dewayne, but we will figure something out."

Later, we learn that every farmer in Hubbard County knew that Dewayne had two big stupid city boys coming to his house who wanted to learn about farming and were willing to help out. We were the most popular newcomers since the Ruby sisters returned home from the Twin Cities.

The Morgan farmhouse is small, but a welcome relief from life on the road. Dewayne's wife Anne is friendly and happy to have someone new to talk to and help around the house. Our first few days are spent midst Anne's yearly bottling of garden vegetables. We steam hundreds of canning bottles and fill them with freshly blanched harvested green beans. Mick is tapped to feed the chickens in the morning and bring in the hens' fresh eggs and I help Dewayne in the barn fixing broken equipment.

On our first full day, Dewayne introduces us to his milk cows. Every morning and evening for the next few months Mick and I will open the barn doors to a line of thirty or so Holsteins, Jerseys and Guernseys waiting to get inside. Milk cows are hierarchical and line up in order of seniority. Cree, a fifteen hundred pound black and white Holstein, is the leader and always enters the barn first. If for some reason Cree arrives late, no one moves until he arrives. When the milking is finished, Cree leaves first followed by each member of the sociable community of sweet bovines. Each produces about 8 to 10 gallons of milk a day and are happy to have their milk sack unburdened.

Some are milked by machines and others by hand and we learn to squeeze the utters from top to bottom in a rhythm that mimics a calves' mouth and tongue around an utter. Before manual milking we fill our palms with a soothing skin gel used to stroke the cows huge milk sack so they drop or release the milk into the utters. They love this milking foreplay and if you forget to do it, they will not drop their milk until you remember. Each member of this troupe has its own unique personality and lets you know what they like and dislike. By the time we leave the farm, I had come to love each one and believed they had an affection for me, too. If I called out to one of my favorites while it grazed in an alfalfa field, it would come running like a fun-loving puppy dog. They look deep and longingly into my eyes with their large expressive brown eyes and I reciprocated, gazing back at them.

One day Mick was telling a joke as we milked and when he got to the punch line he shouted it out for effect. Almost immediately all thirty cows stiffened, lifted their tales and blew gallons of liquid shit across the room, drenching all three of us from head to toe. Standing there with big globs of shit on his face and glasses, Dewayne nonchalantly said, "That's another thing, don't ever make loud noises. Milk cows hate loud noises and quick movements."

After milking one day, Cree stopped at the barn door and refused to leave. She looked into my eyes as if trying to tell me something. The other cows lined up behind her, but Cree would not budge. Dewayne was walking by the barn and saw what was happening and told me that Cree liked to have her forehead rubbed before leaving. I removed my gloves and scratched her forehead between her giant brown eyes.

"That's not going to cut it, Mark," he said. "Try this," Dewayne grabbed Cree by the horns and pulled her enormous head down while at the same time lifting his knee up into the center of her face. He then pulled her head up and down by the horns across his bent knee. When he was finished, Cree looked at him as if saying thanks and quickly left the barn. Every morning and night thereafter, Cree stopped at the door and gave me the eye so I grabbed her by the horns and rubbed her forehead with my knee. Soon, several others stopped in front of me and gave me the hairy eyeball. They too wanted their noggins rubbed.

On our first Saturday morning in Northern Minnesota we woke up on the living room floor where we slept to the sound of people talking and laughing outside in the yard. Looking out the window I see four or five men and the same number of women standing naked on the front lawn waiting their turn to wash themselves down with a hose attached to a big water heater sitting nearby.

Mick and I couldn't take our eyes off one beautiful young woman in the group. She was a dream come true and we were mesmerized. We stood there flatfooted at the window watching and couldn't figure out what was going on so after a while, we sat quietly on the living room couch and watched and waited.

Dewayne finally came in stark naked to get clean clothes,

"Morning," he says, laughing at the sight of us sitting there bug-eyed. "Come on out and join us? Don't you want a bath? I'll introduce you."

"Naked?" Mick asks.

"Don't tell me you couldn't use a bath?" he asked. Looking to me he continues, "Don't tell me *you're* a prude?"

"We weren't sure what to do," I said, thoughtfully. "No one told us anything…"

Interrupting, he continued, "We are the only ones around who still have a working water heater so once a week we get together for coffee and a bath."

We soon learn that Dewayne, Anne and the Saturday bathers are devotees of Rudoph Stiener, the German philosopher, and members of the Rosicrucian Fellowship of the Cosmic Conception. Their farm is one of several whose owners belong to the same church study group.

"Tell me about the Rosicrucians," I ask one morning as we replace a broken plow bottom in the barn.

"Just by asking that question, it means you have evolved to point where you might consider its teachings."

"I might have evolved enough?"

"Just by knowing the church exists means you have advanced in your spiritual journey and now the next move might be learning about its belief system."

"What do you believe?"

"The church is a secret religious and spiritual study group and I am not at liberty to tell you what we study. In fact, the term study group is inaccurate. Each member of the belief system is on his own study program and works individually on courses with the assistance of the Invisible Helpers."

"The invisible what?"

Dewayne ignores my question and asks for a pipe wrench.

The Rosicrucian Fellowship teaches *advanced indi-*

viduals deep insights into Christian mystic philosophy and presents an Astro or virtual meeting ground for religious, scientific and personal beliefs. There are no churches and all course work is accomplished mostly by mail. No one meets its elders or teachers in the conscious realm. Rosicrucians study the Christian bible, have a complex astrological connection and stress self-knowledge and healing through Astro-diagnosis.

Later that evening, Dewayne kicks back in his chair and gazes at his living room ceiling thoughtfully. "Yes, Invisible Helpers, Mark. I can't tell you much more about it because it's for you to explore and discover."

"How does one become a member of the church if it's secret and no one discusses it?"

"Okay, that's a good question. Every week the Los Angeles Times runs a one column inch announcement in the personal ads for those interested in finding out more. The ad includes an address where you can request more information. From there you will be visited in your sleep by the Invisible Helpers. They astral-project to you and ask you specific questions about your beliefs and spiritual needs."

"What?" I say half laughing and totally incredulous. "Astral projecting into my dreams?"

"It's not funny, Mark."

"It seems outrageous!"

"Perhaps to you it might sound that way." He pauses, "Remember you asked me."

"Right. Ignorance is my only redeeming quality."

"If your meeting with the Invisible Helpers goes well and you are on an intersecting spiritual or soulful path, they leave you with a clear light recollection of their visit and with an address to respond to. If you are not ready, you will remember nothing."

Dewayne retrieves an old LA Times newspaper sitting under a pile of magazines and bills and drops it into my lap.

A few days later, after several days bailing and stacking hay for Roger, I go through the hundreds of ads in the Times and find a small personal ad that starts with the word Rosicrucian. I pull a post card from my pack, address it to the listed post office box address in Los Angeles, borrow a stamp from Anne and drop it in the mailbox.

The next Saturday morning Mick and I are up early, ready but anxious for the naked public bath. We find Dewayne in the bathroom with a hammer. He stands back and hits the toilet hard and squarely. The upper half collapses into several large pieces and crashes to the floor. He then hits the bottom half with authority and it too, breaks into many pieces.

Dewayne explains that modern plumbing is evil and that toilets take us away from the simple life where we need to face all our humanity.

"From now on when you do your business," he says, "go out to the field I plowed yesterday and leave your offering in one of the furrows."

We are speechless.

"Questions?"

"Not really," Mick says. "It's your house."

"Nitrogen is the best fertilizer anywhere."

So from that day forward, when I needed to do my business I'd grab a roll of toilet paper and squat among the plowed furrows.

About 9 am the bathers arrive and Anne introduces us to everyone as we strip down and wait our turn under the warm hose. Neither Mick nor I had been anywhere near a beautiful young woman – let alone naked – in a long time and we struggle to avert our eyes at the proper moments. As we wait, Monica, Dewayne's three-year-old daughter who likes call herself "the naked baby," stands next to Anne and sizes up the men. Turning to her mother, she points to Mick's member and loudly asks, "Mommy, why does Mickey have a little boy's wiener when Mark and Daddy have a big boy's wiener?"

A laugh goes up and Mick's face turns beet-red and he cups his unit with both hands. Anne nonchalantly replies, "Monica, some boys have big thingies and others have little ones."

For the next few months, the peace I feel at the farm is something I've never experienced before. The mornings and evenings are soothing and sublime and while we work hard almost every day as loggers or farm hands there is a deep sense of belonging to something much larger. I am no longer at the center of this universe, but I feel I'm an integral part of it and it is part of me.

This land of farms and lakes and forests buries itself deep into my heart and the feeling I felt as a boy back home in the 1950s at the Taylor house washes over me and I am at home again. The anxiety and gnawing of city life seem far away and I am unencumbered and whole. After dinner in the evenings, Mick and I sit outside in the farmyard and read or talk about buying or renting a place somewhere nearby. We practice Frisbee and when we miss one, Lobo, the family dog, is happy to return it to us. Sometimes at dusk we walk through the empty fields into the forest where we might see a deer or hear timber wolves calling out to the moon.

CHAPTER SEVENTEEN

RIO VERDE

2018

Deciding a shower might calm me down, I find some much needed relief under the warm and comforting water. Leaning hard against the tiled wall with the water luxuriously rushing over me, I let my hand move over my chest where my left breast and nipple once existed. I run my finger along the line of the incision from my sternum to my armpit. It is numb and sensitive. My hand then moves across my flat belly and down between my legs. Suddenly, I realize my balls are missing! "What the fuck?" I say aloud. "Where in the hell…"

Panicked, I jump from the shower and stand in front of the mirror, searching the bag of my scrotum for my balls with my fingertips. Nothing. Are my testes so traumatized by the chemo poisoning they've sought sanctuary up inside my torso? I remember a fistfight in my youth where an opponent kicked me in the nuts and later that night, I found a bulge in my lower abdomen. It was my balls!

Finally, after some searching, I find what was left of my nuts. My beautiful egg-shaped balls that once were rock hard and larger than the giant Cerignola olives grown in Israel are now tiny, soft and squishy. They are the size of small sickly grapes. I press one between my thumb and forefinger until I fear it might burst – surprisingly there is no pain. My gonads are dead. My fucking balls are dead! My proud package and the one-time director of my every adolescent move have succumbed. Chemo killed them. I have betrayed my own manhood – my own body – for the illusive promise of a few low quality days at the end of my life.

In the bedroom, I lie across the bed and sob. How could I let this happen? How could I have fallen this far? Before I can consider an answer, the intense pain surfaces again. I can't breathe and the luxurious bed against my back makes my muscles contract and seize. I rock from side to side; hip-to-hip in a movement that has become second nature. I sit in a comfortable oversized leather chair, but never stop moving, changing from one position to another. I can't breathe so I move out onto the patio where I realize my eyes are aching and burning. I had no idea what bone pain was until now. The chemo has killed my precious nuts and is now attacking the cancer in my bones. My hips, legs, feet, ribs and skull ache. Later, in the middle of the night, I walk up and down the driveway for hours attempting to overcome the muscle spasms, nausea, upset stomach, heartburn and outrageous pain in my jaw. Pausing under my studio door light, I piss into the gravel and the flow is thick beige-colored foam. It bubbles up into a ball, higher and higher until it's about a foot high. It's the consistency of heavy whipping cream, and reminds me of my mother's famous Thanksgiving fruit salad. It would be funny if it weren't so profoundly depressing.

I learned after my diagnosis that I am not a cancer warrior, not one of those people who take their diagnosis in stride and start a blog about cures and ideas for others also going down the shit tube. I have accepted my diagnosis, but would spring into action if there was something tangible I might do to thwart it. I have seen and read of cancer warriors who relentlessly and with honest enthusiasm have engaged the fight. People whose spirited fearlessness has supposedly kept them alive and healthy far longer than anyone in the medical community suspected. It is not that I have caved and thrown my arms up in defeat. I just can't face the notion that hope and attitude will change the course of my cancer or kill off the sucker cancer cells.

I read somewhere that cancer is a force of nature that acts within the human body, just as the winds and rains from a hurricane are forces of nature that act on the earth. We are insignificant and powerless in the face of these unleashed forces. There comes a time when we must admit to this powerlessness and evacuate ahead of the deadly hurricane, rather than remain behind and make some kind of empty symbolic anaerobic gesture. Similarly, there comes a time when one must recognize the futility of continuing the personal physical fight against cancer, when chemo is no longer a desirable option, when one should begin the process of saying goodbye and understand that death is not the enemy, but merely the next part of life.

Some days I feel desperate to be *me* again… or hope I might explode into a billion molecules and drift away into the invisible world of atoms and dark matter.

Until then I will remain strong, but at some point I will march out of my mental and psychological safe house and win my battle. While I may not be a hopeful cancer warrior, I will always be a warrior. There is a cure for incurable cancer: death. I will win over its insidious march forward. I will stop it in its tracks. And a few minutes after my glorious battle has been won, a few minutes after my heart stops and my brain ceases its righteous supremacy, my cancers will die, too. Those gone-crazy cancer cells will shrivel up and be turned to dust and they will never assault me again. I am a warrior and I will run against my own blade to win this war.

I have experienced so much disappointment as my body shuts down and rejects itself, I've needed to cry - to just sit down and cry. My best friend, Grant, came to Rio and he and I have always had deep and meaningful conversations about love and life, but I could not speak of these things as I had always done because the tears and a deep growing primal howl would have rushed out and destroyed it all. I'm supposed to be smart, stoic and strong. After eight days of trying Grant left and went home and we had never crossed that valley to the joyful communications that has been a hallmark of our friendship and love.

This pain and suffering will decide when I die. I have promised myself not to wait too long before taking myself out. If my spinal tumors destroy a vertebrae and cause paralysis, it will be too late. I need to be vigilant and to be early and not late. It is okay to discuss this with you because you understand that one day – sometime in the future – you too may face this situation. The more you contemplate it, the easier it becomes to discuss and make a plan for its undoing.

Pain will decide. Perhaps pain is there to make us know that trying to survive no longer suffices. It wears you down with a constant, unrelenting efficiency. The pain will decide.

I am committed to dying with dignity, with the idea that my life mattered and that I am now following the inexorable path we all must take.

My commitment is easy; I want to die on my own terms. No one wants to die, even though they want the pain to stop, but I will not waste away in some nursing home or leave it to Lana to take care of me while tearing her heart out with each new day until the end. I want to stand and face the elements – the land, the horizon, the endless sky, and the never-ending space above. My terms are simple and doable. But I must take my leave a bit early so I can make it happen the way I need it to be.

CHAPTER EIGHTEEN

HOLLYWOOD, CALIFORNIA

2019

The flight to Burbank is uneventful except on landing I'm surprised to find the airport is a Walt Disney 1950s throwback. I can't remember the last time I disembarked a plane using a staircase to the tarmac. The interior of the building can be summed up in one word: rectilinear. In my mind, I see Pan Am stewardesses dressed in blue and white and wearing white gloves and that distinctive pill-box cap strolling the concourse.

The sky is overcast with marine layer and a sodium bouquet of the Pacific. I take a cab around the Hollywood Hills and along Franklin Avenue to the Scientology Celebrity Centre. A day earlier I received a call with instructions to come to Hollywood immediately. All the arrangements were made, my flight booked, a room at the storied Celebrity Center, and after checking-in, a car would take me to the Scientology Media Productions (SMP) compound.

The Celebrity Centre is an impressive piece of Victorian architecture sitting at the center of Hollywood. Constructed of Italian white marble blocks, it could be the last surviving palace built by the first generation of big name moviemakers and film industry titans.

Financed by William Randolph Hurst, it was built for the widow of a business associate who mysteriously died on Hurst's yacht in 1924 during a wild drunken party. Many believe famed actor Charlie Chaplin shot the man when he confronted Chaplin attempting to seduce his wife. Hurst was said to have felt responsible and built the impressive structure to serve as luxurious residential apartments for members of the film community and as a source of income for the grieving widow.

Originally named the Chateau Elysee, it was a replica of a seventeenth century French castle. The architect, Arthur Harvey, designed Hurst's famous northern California castle San Simeon. A generation later, the Chateau became the Manor Hotel and housed some of the greatest Hollywood stars of the day. Error Flynn, Bette Davis, Clark Gable, Katharine Hepburn, George Gershwin, Ginger Rogers and Humphrey Bogart all lived there. The Manor hosted lavish parties and every night residents gathered in the dining room for dinner, drinks and socializing.

I'm in room 609, a two-floor suite that was home to George Burns and Gracie Allen for fifteen years. The first floor is spacious with a comfortable living room, large windows and a kitsch 1940s kitchen. A steep and wide stairway leads to the luxurious bedroom and bathroom on the second floor. A sitting area occupies a large nook with facing windows overlooking the Hollywood hills. The suite is obviously meant for VIPs and I wonder what I'm doing here.

A call comes in from John Sugg. "Where are you?"

"At the hotel."

"A car is out front - waiting." Sugg is the executive editor of Freedom Magazine.

"I see. I'll be right there."

At the secured SMC (Scientology Media Center) on Sunset Boulevard the offices of Freedom Magazine are empty except for Sugg who sits in his sunny corner office suite and is on the phone. Until my recent book assignment, I was a senior investigative writer and had an office here. I was one of sixteen writers – two with Pulitzers – who were contracted to breathe new life into the magazine, which had been in an on-again, off-again hiatus for several years. Five offices sit adjacent to Sugg's and none has an assigned occupant. Like me, most contributors work remotely and only make it into the office occasionally so when in town, we pick an office and make it our own. I pick one next to the conference room furthest from Sugg and log onto my computer.

"What are *you* doing here?" John Sugg asks as he appears in the doorway.

"Good to see you too, John," I feign hurt. "You tell me, what *AM I* doing here?

"I have no idea."

Chuckling, "I was summoned and that's all I know."

John has been angry since I was plucked from his staff to generate the attack on the Scientologist book and was no longer assigned to the magazine. I was working on several high priority investigative projects and had been forced to table them.

"The only thing I know is," John concedes, "Bill Walsh wants a face to face with you." John raises his eyebrows and drops his shoulders.

"Care to speculate?"

"It's not good," John laughs and changes the subject, "How's the book going?"

"Trying to absorb 70 plus years of history and its endless nuances – then regurgitate it back with authority and style has its challenges."

Sugg smirks, "Loads of bullshit, too…"

"I'm meeting Bill here?"

"How the fuck would I know?" He turns to leave, "Ask Donna, she asked me to give you a call at the Manor."

Donna is one of the church executives whose role is to thwart any attempt to displace or dislodge her. Many church officials have been here for decades and are inordinately focused on holding their place. I dial her up.

"Donna, Mark Taylor here."

"Oh hi Mark. Are you at SMC?"

"Indeed. What's the plan?"

"Well, I'm waiting to hear from Bill…" she hesitates as if distracted.

"Walsh?" I finish for her.

"Yes, he's flying in from DC and wants to meet. Hold tight, I'll try to reach him or his assistant."

An hour later, Donna calls back. "Bill is still in DC. He apologizes and wants you to wait."

"Any idea when he'll be here?"

"Late tonight or midday tomorrow. I'm not sure."

On my way out, I stop at John's office but his door is locked. I can hear him hollering at someone on the phone.

The next morning, after spending the previous night feeling Burns and Allen's latent energy lounging around and repeating George's famous, "Say goodnight Gracie," while pretending to smoke a big stogy, I have room service deliver poached eggs, toast and coffee to my room. I walk the mile or so along Sunset Boulevard to the Scientology Media Center. Walsh left a late voicemail saying he had arrived and to meet him in the morning.

After clearing SMC security, including a Malinois Belgian guard dog, I decide to check out the historic property. Opened in 1912, the movie studio and now state-of-the-art media center is the oldest continuously operated film studio in Hollywood. On my tour I stop at a soundstage where the huge doors are open and a crew is filming segments of a documentary with semi-autonomous robotic movie cameras. I step inside quietly and stand along a back wall. The room is massive and dark and I'm filled with a sense of wonder and magic. In 1938 this soundstage hosted the creation of scenes from The Wizard of Oz.

When Bill arrives, we meet in the Freedom conference room and he tells me about his recent trips to Spain and New Zealand with church leader David Miscavige to help the church clear regulatory problems on the purchase of historic pieces of architecture destined to house Scientology community centers.

He finally breeches the subject of why we are here.

"How's the book proceeding?"

"The book is going well overall, but as I mentioned in my email and during our last call, I'm having difficulty finding the Hubbard quotes for Chapter Two."

"Chapter Two is important, it's pivotal," Bill interrupts, "perhaps the most important chapter of the book."

"Most people say they know about Hubbard's speeches and quotes or have read them, but despite repeated requests no one has supplied me with copies of them. Everyone refers me to someone else."

"Yeah, I've asked around and I'm hoping I can help you out. How important are they to the piece?"

"Imperative. They are the substantiation to making the case that Hubbard not only outed the CIA and psychiatry, but also led the campaign to get the information out to the public. We have one excellent excerpt from his second book and a couple of minor quotes, but if he made repeated and ongoing references to the mind control experiments of the 1950s we need to have the locations, dates and transcripts to prove it."

"Okay, okay, let me see what I can do." Bill dials up Karen Pouw, one of the most powerful executives in the Church.

"Karen, Bill Walsh. Yes, got in last night. Hey, remember the conversation about Mr. Hubbard's quotes and the CIA and mind control stuff? Yes... yes... you said... yes... Okay. I'll give him a call. Thanks. "

Pouw refers him to Richard Wieland, a church historian. I don't want to tell Walsh that I've been working with Wieland and he has been tremendously helpful, but he referred me to someone in archives who never called me back or returned my emails. Walsh dials Wieland up.

"Richard, Bill Walsh here. Say, I've got Mark Taylor here. He's... yes, you've talked to him? Have you got the quotes? Okay, see what you can do, thanks. Call me back..."

"The chapter probably would not hold up in court without them, either." Bill says thoughtfully. "Any way of working around it?"

"There are always ways to work around things. The easiest is by simply not including anything... but that won't work here. It's part of the church ethos and history... And why should we work around it? The quotes exist, right?"

Bill interrupts me to take an incoming call. Afterward he says,

"There is someone who would like to meet you. He might be able to help."

Bill calls for a car and a black Chevrolet stretch Suburban limousine with dark tinted windows pull past security and swings around in front of us.

A large man in a black suit gets out of the passenger front and opens the back door for me. Bill pushes past me and I slide in afterwards. The driver is attired in a pressed black suit and appears as if he could be an ex-football player.

Bill is on another call. When finished he says, "Dave tries to keep people from finding out where he works, so we are going to drive around until we are certain no one is following us."

I have been waiting for something like this – straight out of Mission Impossible. I've been invited to events where Miscavige and Tom Cruise were present, but I declined for one reason or another. Some people are drawn to celebrity while others are repelled by it, I fall into the latter category.

Twenty minutes later we pull up in front of a ten or fifteen story historic skyscraper on Hollywood Boulevard near the iconic Capital Records Building. The door opens and we climb out into a crowd of onlookers. The sidewalk is black marble and Walk of Fame stars are situated every ten or twenty feet. We are at the center of tourist Hollywood. The onlookers are trying to figure out who we are. I want to tell them, 'Hey, don't waste your time I'm a nobody.' Two uniformed security men exit the building and escort us into the building's foyer and lock the door behind us.

"This is one of Dave's hideouts," Bill says entering one of three elevators. "This elevator goes to the very top."

We exit into a large open area with wall-to-wall windows, couches and chairs and shelves of books. Richard Wieland, the church historian is waiting, as are other executives. They are waiting their turn to see Miscavige. Bill opens one of the other offices and invites me in.

"We will have more privacy here."

The office is an executive suite and has a spectacular view of the city. A large desk commands the room and many trophies and family photographs sit on polished wooden shelving. The desk appears as if its occupant just stepped out. A nameplate on the desk reads: Heber Carl Jentzsch, President of the Church of Scientology.

"Oh yeah," Wieland notices me looking, "this is Heber's office. He retired not long ago."

Wieland has a large legal folder and hands it to me.

I thank him, sit down in a leather side chair and quickly scan the documents. Meanwhile, Bill disappears into Miscavige's office. When he returns he informs me we might be in for a long wait because everything is taking longer than scheduled.

After reviewing the file, I lamely ask, "Am I missing

something? I don't see any new material or quotes or references to speeches or really anything new."

Surprised Wieland asks, "Can I see that?"

I handed the file to him and he and Walsh goes through it together.

"I specifically asked the archive's department to give me all the Hubbard quotes," Wieland says, looking up at me. Walsh is incredulous.

"Shit, this can't be all of it! It's a mistake." Walsh walks to the window, "We will get to the bottom of this."

There is an uneasy silence as we wait. After about an hour while I scan news sites on my Iphone and Bill makes calls relating to other court matters in Washington, I hear voices and some commotion in the foyer. Oddly, one of the voices sounds familiar to me. A few minutes later after Walsh ends his call, he leaves and returns ten minutes later. As he left the room, he left the door partially open and I see David Miscavige and Tom Cruise standing near the elevator. Walsh catches them and they lean forward and talk in hushed tones for a few minutes.

When he returns, he has a look of practiced shock on his face.

"There isn't going to be a meeting. Dave had an important development. He and Tom left a few minutes ago."

On our way down in the elevator, Bill says, "Mark, I need some help from you, there are a few things we need to discuss. There are a few facts we can't put in the book. Remember when Hubbard told people that he had been asked to become an FBI agent?"

I nodded, "Yes, it was something else I was going to enquire about."

"That really never happened." He paused for effect. "Sometimes Ron exaggerated – as we all do – and he was, how should I say it, something of a bullshitter. There are a few other minor issues we need to discuss, you and I… I'm going to get you the quotes you need and we are going to move forward. This is between you and I. I hope I can trust you on this matter."

"Sure Bill," I say, not understanding fully what was taking place.

"I know Dave really wants to meet you. As long as you can put this book together in a compelling and truthful way and the big guy then Okays it, the sky is the limit for you. You can write your own paycheck. I've read your work, it's good."

As the elevator door opens, he shakes my hand and tells the driver to take me wherever I want to go.

"I'll be in touch soon."

"Thanks, Bill. Talk to you soon."

Bill disappears into the elevator, and the limo driver delivers me back to the Manor Hotel where I have a leisurely highball sitting on Errol Flynn's favorite stool at the bar.

CHAPTER NINETEEN

SALT LAKE CITY AND BATON ROUGE
AUGUST 1989

It was deadline week and NEO Magazine was about to go to press. I hadn't collected all the checks from last issue's advertisers and was frantically was trying to raise the money needed to pay my printer. Most of my advertisers were small businesses, boutiques, restaurants, art galleries, performing arts institutions and individual artists who could ill-afford to advertise, but could not survive without it. Many had taken a chance on my fledgling art publication so I gave them as much time as I could to pay.

NEO published art and literary art and was designed in a stunning, oversized, black and white periodical format that found almost immediate success with the downtown urban art, intellectual, university set. The title NEO was short for Neologism, a word introduced to me by Mick when we were on the road. A neologism is the formation of new words and phrases from existing words and phrases. On occasions Mick mixed words or phrases together creating funny new words and meanings.

Once when we were hitchhiking from Denver to New Mexico and riding in the back of a pick-up truck, Mick said, "I need to piss so bad my weenis hurts."

I laughed loudly and repeated, "Weenis? Where'd that come from?"

Mick had combined weenie and penis to create weenis. When my laughter died away I noticed his mood darkened and after a long silence said his psychiatrist told him this strange ability to create new words – neologisms - was a symptom of his mental illness.

Publishing a bi-monthly magazine is quite a trick. In my case, I had sixty days to put an issue together, have it printed and distributed. I used my own money to get the first issue out and for the next two years I was the only employee and didn't take a dime out, plowing every cent back into the business. While I made nothing I ate in excellent restaurants and had tickets to every performance in the city. The truth is, small publications live and die on advertising trade. Later when NEO took-off I insisted on more cash. I did however trade the magazine's back cover for a year's lease on a million dollar condo perched on the mountainside above Main Street in Park City. While my friends and family ate at the best restaurants and had the best and most pricy seats for art performances, I still needed $10,000 in cash every sixty days to get an issue out.

But in the early days, every dime counted and sometimes I had to go collect past due revenue. On this day I drove to the Tower Theater, an art film house, where the owner Adam was in a similar hand to mouth situation. He lived in the theater's projection room and sold old and donated videos to make ends meet.

Adam owed me over $1000 and I hadn't seen a payment in nine months. He was avoiding me and everyone he owed money to. When I arrived at 9 am I caught him unlocking the front door to leave. He spotted me coming and quickly slipped back inside and was trying to lock me out when I pushed my way into the foyer.

"Adam, this has got to stop," I told him. "I can't wait or chase you around any longer. I need a check and I need it now."

"I don't have it."

"I've run your ads for months without a payment. I'll be forced to pull your new ad."

"Fuck you, Mark."

I stiffen. It's one thing not getting paid for a service

you provided, but another having someone tell you to fuck off for having the audacity of asking for payment.

"Listen, if you weren't such a little fuck I'd take your head off right now!" I moved in closer. Adam is five feet and nine inches tall and 140 pounds and I'm six foot three and two hundred pounds. As a younger man I had many fights and could hold my own.

"Fuck you," he repeated. "Go ahead, kick the shit out of me if you want, I don't have the money. If I did, you wouldn't even be on my list, so fuck you again."

I step back, "I see. Adam. People told me not to trust you. Your reputation sucks and now you won't have any way to promote your upcoming films."

"As if I didn't know that…" he smirked.

I move closer again. My muscles tighten and I decide to knock the shit out of him if he insults me one more time. He was smart and realized I wouldn't stand for much more abuse before taking action.

"I guess I'll just have to go under. Fuck everyone!" he yelled, moving back and forth and turning in circles. "What am I supposed to do?" He was crying now. "The house is half empty every night and I can't pay rent or staff. They all quit!"

I left and drove to Liberty Park to settle out my anger

before going on to Voila! a gift shop owned by my friend and advertiser Joe Pitti.

"Mark," Joe said, smiling as I entered. "Good to see you. How's the next issue coming?"

"The issue is looking good. I hope people love it."

Joe moved around a counter near the cash register and pulled out an envelope and handed it to me. "Thanks for the extra time on this."

Inside was a $750 check. I was relieved. "No problem, Joe, I wish everyone was as honest as you."

I told him about Adam at the Tower and he commiserated. "I don't know why we do it, retail or small business. It sucks us dry."

After small talking for half an hour I return to my office at ArtSpace. Waiting for me is the project director, Steven Goldsmith.

"Mark," he said, "Glad I caught you."

I knew why he was there. "Come on up Steven, I've got the rent for you."

"Great!" he seems genuinely relieved. "Utah Power just sent me a turn off notice - $1200 by today!"

"Holy shit!"

After Goldsmith leaves, I settle in to finish an editorial when my phone rings.

"Mark Taylor," I answer.

"Mark Taylor?" the voice asks.

"Yes. Speaking. Who do I have the pleasure of speaking with?"

"Mark, this is Larry… Larry Flynt, you know. Allan McDonald told me about you. He said you are willing to take the assignment you two discussed."

"Larry!" I answer, startled. "Yes sir. I'm very interested in this assignment. It's nice to speak to you. There are some details that need…"

"Okay, Mark," he interrupts, "I just want to touch bases with you personally. When do you think you can get started?"

"Well, I publish an art journal here and this is deadline week. How about sometime in the next two weeks?"

"Okay, good. Here, talk to Emily my assistant, she will send the contract and a check for the 25% upfront money you've requested. She can make all the travel arrangements, too."

Most of my income came from writing features for national magazines and I had been negotiating with Allan McDonald, Editor-in-Chief of Hustler Magazine, for months on a 6-month undercover assignment. After several rounds of discussions I concluded it wasn't going to happen and then whammo, out of the blue, the assignment has materialized and they were posting a $10,000 check by FedEx. Life is good. My temporary financial problems just evaporated, but now I faced a larger problem: how was I going to continue publishing NEO while assuming a new identity and going undercover fifteen hundred miles away to investigate one of America's foremost cable satellite televangelists, Jimmy Swaggart?

A week later I boarded a flight to Baton Rouge, ready to start my new undercover assignment. I kept this assignment quiet and few even knew I left town. NEO's new issue was out and it gave me a couple of weeks to figure out how to operate and catch the lay of the land in Louisiana. My closest associates in Utah asked how I was going to proceed and I answered with the truth, "I really don't know. I'll figure it out when I get there."

No good writer likes to be unprepared but my professional life was busier than it had ever been and I didn't have the luxury of contemplation or basic preparation. But as fate and luck would have it, I got my first lead, although I discounted it at the time, from the taxicab driver that took me to my hotel near the state capital.

"First time to Baton Rouge?" Clarence, the middle

aged African American man asked, as we drove through the darkness and intense humidity.

"I'm here on business," I said, "and looking forward to checking out the town."

He laughs, "I think you best head south to Nawlins if you are looking for night life. We pretty much roll up the sidewalk 'round here by 10 p.m."

Since I had nothing to lose, I added, "Actually, I'm a writer here doing a story on Jimmy Swaggart."

"Whew!" he said. "Man, you be nuts."

"Why is that, you know about Swaggart?"

"Everyone around these parts knows about Mr. Swaggart. He owns half the houses in town."

"He's a landlord, too?"

"Yeah and a damned mean one at that."

"I don't know squat," I admit and introduce myself as Randall Potts.

"Well," Clarence responded, "folks don't like Mr. Swaggart here abouts much. I mean he's got his churches and all his followers, but he's someone you don't go messin' with, if you know what I mean. Nasty."

Half chuckling, I answer, "Really? I've caught a few of his cable shows and he seems like a good-old Christian boy."

"Yeah, like all 'dem Christians, out and about on Saturday night and praisin' Jesus on Sunday morning."

At the hotel, I got Clarence's card and told him I was in need of a good driver to show me around. I asked if he would keep our conversation to himself. He nodded, "Yes sir."

"If you were a writer looking for information or dirt on Swaggart, where would you turn?" I enquire.

"Well, Mr. Potts, you probably know a lot about the goings on in your hometown since you were raised there, and people here know a lot about Swaggart that no one talks about. From what I hear you better be spending time looking at Swaggart's extra-curricular activities down on Airport highway in Nawlins. I hear he spends a lot of time on the down low there."

Over the next few months, I travel between Baton Rouge and Salt Lake City. There are long days at the court-house in Baton Rouge and at the Times Picayune Newspaper archives in New Orleans going through reams of microfiche (long before the internet and access to the world's vast trove of archival materials). In Baton Rouge I become a member of Swaggart's congregation and attend Sunday worship services.

I had chosen the name Randall Potts because Randall

was my best friend in school who passed away mysteriously in 1977. I knew everything there was to know about him: his age, social security number and complete family history. The entire time I borrowed his identity no one questioned me. Even today, I have a social media account in Randall's name and use it for research.

Back in Salt Lake I was becoming a minor celebrity because people in Utah who were not part of the Mormon experience felt lost or invisible with no one representing them or speaking to them. NEO found an audience whose voice had not been acknowledged or heard. NEO published smart articles, short stories, poetry, editorials and art exhibitions. It possessed the feel of something of value and each issue contained substantive writing and intellectual subjects. In an article published by the New York Times Magazine about the competition between rival art magazines in the Manhattan area, NEO was mentioned for being one of the best new art publications out in America's hinterlands.

I spent half my time in Utah researching Swaggart, his Assemblies of God congregation and its college campus on Bluebonnet Road, and half my time in Baton Rouge assigning stories, writing editorials and working with NEO's talented art directors in Salt Lake City.

While most remember Jimmy Swaggart for his dalliances with Debra Murphree, the prostitute in New Orleans' seedy Airport Road neighborhood – which I helped uncover and expose – Swaggart's real enterprise was a quarter of a billion dollars a year bait-and-switch house of cards. He raised hundreds of millions from viewers for orphaned children living in the streets of Central America. Much of that money did help build homes and schools for the less fortunate, but the majority of money disappeared into a general operating fund bank account that he used as his personal piggy bank. Because he paid no taxes, he built a college and a huge complex of schools and training facilities on Bluebonnet Road. He bought real estate and his representatives had twenty ways you might leave your house and estate to his church, but continue to live in house until you died. He guaranteed estate holders a hallowed place in the halls of heaven. He was the single biggest landlord in the south owning more than 1100 single dwellings and hundreds of commercial buildings.

During my investigation I discovered that Swaggart paid one particular printing company millions of dollars to supply him with brochures and books and every kind of promotional material. When I asked the owner of another printing company why he had none of Swaggart's business he calmly told me, "Because I refuse to offer the kickbacks he demands."

Here's how it worked. If Swaggart Ministries needed one hundred thousand booklets and the competitive bids from printers in the area came in around one million dollars, the printer who got the bid - and all of his printing business - would be the high bidder at $2.5 million. Why would anyone pay an extra 1.5 million for a job it could get for one million? The answer is simple, the printer had a deal to kick back half of the overpayment to Swaggart in cash. This money would go straight into his or his son's personal accounts. No one knew any better and this arrangement went on for years. Good investigators look at suppliers of services the subject is doing business with and at the same time, talk to the competition to see what they have to say.

On Thanksgiving after being in Baton Rouge on and off for three months, a fellow parishioner who I met at a Swaggart congregation men's group, invited me to dinner with his family. I was taken aback by this gracious act of kindness. I was alone and feeling down. My father was in the hospital for a heart attack that would eventually kill him.

When I arrived at the house I was greeted with warmth

and treated like family. When the table was all set and the turkey sat on a huge platter at the center of the table and the extended family bowed their heads in a blessing, I watched and felt like an imposter, a spy and a liar whose betrayal was cheap and dishonest. I was there to work my way into people's confidence. I broke bread with these good people because they were good Christians – both kind and compassionate.

A woman I met there, an attractive divorcee, offered to introduce me to the 'Singles' group at the congregation. Over the next month I attended get-togethers at a nearby bowling alley and meetings at people's homes. I learned that Swaggart relied on single people with more disposable income and time to help with fundraising. Singles were a highly valued resource and soon I found myself donating my time helping with clerical work in Swaggart's office building on the same floor as his spacious personal office.

After a four-month undercover investigation I surfaced in Baton Rouge and New Orleans as an investigative journalist working on a Swaggart expose. By the time I went public I knew all about Swaggart's weekly visits to the ten-dollar prostitute Debra Murphree and about his scamming the elderly out of their savings and estates. His enemies came out of the woodwork and filled in the blanks of his duplicity and law breaking.

Back in Salt Lake City, I was stopped on the sidewalk by a woman carrying a copy of NEO. She was furious. I had met this person a few times in passing at art functions and knew her son was a promising actor.

"Mark," she exclaimed, "I can't believe you'd run a feature article in NEO saying that if you have talent and you live out in what the writer (I was the writer) calls the "hinterlands" it is essential to move to New York City or Los Angeles if you want any chance at success!"

NEO had indeed run a feature about The Kitchen, the New York City experimental art organization that helps young and newly arrived artists from communities with fewer professional opportunities to find work. The Kitchen was housed in a huge building gifted by a rich art patron and included theaters for playwrights, choreographers and dancers, studio space for painters and sculptors, cinemas, a nightclub and even apartments for promising newcomers. The piece basically said if you want to see what you've got it, you should leave home and test yourself in the Big Apple. To paraphrase the old saying, 'If you can make it there, you can make it anywhere.' If you don't do this, you will never know if you can make it in the business of art or not.

Apparently, this woman's son quit his job in Utah and was now living on the streets of Manhattan unable to find work or anyone who might believe in his talent. In conclusion she admonished me, "Mark, you have to consider the impact NEO has on young artists!"

Before she stormed off, I commented that I stood by the piece and remarked that whatever experience her son might find in New York City, it would most likely be a positive and cherished experience (if he survives). I concluded by saying, "He can always come home and live with you."

A block or two away I ran into another artist, a talented art director and painter, who ran up to me, threw her arms around my neck and gave me a big hug.

"Mark! Mark! Thank you!" She went on, "the piece about The Kitchen made me catch a flight to New York where I spent two weeks peddling my portfolio around and I landed my dream job at MOMA in the art department! Can you believe it?"

She continued, "Without that kick in the butt, I would have stayed here, living at my folks' house and selling my work for peanuts! Thank you, thank you!"

I was flabbergasted and refused to take credit. "Wonderful. I'm so happy for you! It had nothing to do with me and everything to do with you and the talent you possess."

She was back in town to finish packing and pick up her sister who was moving with her. When she walked away I was on cloud nine and realized each individual takes what they will or can from the information they read and I'd just experienced the best and worst of what the printed word can accomplish.

Now back in Salt Lake, I reconnected with everyone involved with NEO. Since its premiere two years earlier I'd become friends with a large cadre of the city's art community.

One of the people I wanted to reconnect with was Joe Pitti, the owner of Voila! We often shared lunch or met for dinner, sometimes spending hours discussing the problems and possible solutions for the art communities' dilemmas and listening to each other's stories about the difficulty living in a monoculture, a place where the Mormon Church decides how the rest of us should live.

A nationally recognized mime, Joe landed in Utah after taking a temporary job teaching at the theater department of the University of Utah. After his job at the University ended, Joe was hit particularly hard by the funding inequity imposed by the Utah Arts Council and struggled to make ends meet. He studied with Marcel Marceau in Paris and was a principal performer with the Harold Clurman Theatre in New York City. He had even performed at Carnegie Hall, but he had never experienced an art community that generously funded the traditional historic arts such as Ballet West, the Utah Symphony and the Utah Opera Company while turning its back on individual contemporary artists. When we met he was destitute and needed rent money. A friend in New York came to his rescue, loaned him a few thousand dollars and he opened Voila! a specialty gift shop.

A few months or so after my return I began to see a slow change in Joe's personality. His effervescence diminished and he became increasingly dark and melancholy. When I asked him about it he told me David, his lover, was dying of AIDS. At the time, the AIDS epidemic was full throttle and thousands of gay men were dying each year.

He confided that every week David was weaker and weaker and had fallen into a deep depression. His illness would soon force him to stop working and he had developed a plan to take his life when his savings ran out and he could no longer pay his bills. He was adamant that he would not be a burden to Joe or his family. As Joe told me this, his face was a study of anguish and he was flushed with fear.

Over the next few months, Joe canceled lunches and

dinners and I grew increasingly uneasy. During the day he managed the shop so I often stopped by just to say hello and see how he was doing. On one visit Joe seemed even more down than usual.

"David quit his job," he told me, "and he is barely able to get around the apartment." He said David talked more often about implementing his plan to end his life. He decided to do it at the point he became bedridden.

Every time I saw Joe I tried to be upbeat, inviting him out to eat, offering concert tickets or just sitting quietly and listening. I tried consoling him, but felt I was of little help.

A few weeks later, Joe called and wanted to meet for lunch at the busy Rio Grande Café. I was happy to hear his voice and thought things might be somehow better.

I arrived at the café first and when he caught me looking at him coming through the door he struck the pose of a beautiful Hollywood ingénue sashaying forward, all hips and shoulders and taking tiny steps as if wearing a long designer dress with a matching clutch purse. He blushed as if embarrassed and I rocked back and forth in laughter.

I expected he needed to ventilate, but was surprised because he seemed happier and at peace. He told me he begged David not to take his life and David relented, saying he was still going to kill himself because he hated what life had become, but he would wait until he went blind.

The next time we met a month or two later, Joe was worse than ever and experiencing what I would call profound depression. But there was something else too, I sensed a mixture of anger and frustration and the story he told was even more bizarre.

David had been bedridden for two months and had gone blind, but decided to wait to implement his plan until after the holidays so he could say goodbye to all his loved ones. In early January his mother wanted to visit one last time so he decided to wait until after her visit to do the deed. In the meantime, Joe was growing more and more exhausted and was an emotional mess. He lost weight and was not eating. But when David's mother left and the appointed day arrived nothing happened. Joe was afraid to ask what the new plan was but when David found the strength he told him he would wait until the weather broke and spring arrived. This would be the final deadline and no more delays. Springtime in the mountain west does not arrive on a particular day so several proposed dates came and went and David became sicker and just kept announcing one date after another. All of this wore Joe down and he fell ill with exhaustion and his doctor wanted to admit Joe to a hospital.

During this period, Joe was working full time, rehearsing and performing and was David's only caretaker. After so many monumental death dates, Joe became weary and only half listened when David announced a new date and swore that this time it was really going to happen.

One morning before he left for work, David asked Joe if he would stop at the store and bring him some ice cream. Joe was in a hurry but rushed off. When he returned, David was sitting up in his bed dead.

David wanted to have control over his life and death. For those who have been given a terminal diagnosis and who every day are forced to experience death's inexorable march forward, it's an easy concept to understand. Death is going to take you sooner or later, but you still want to exert some control over *your own life* – and decide when and where it happens. Sadly no one knows when the right time arrives.

I feel as David did. I have a plan and the means to take my life. When my health reaches an unspecified and undefined point of deterioration I will implement my plan. Until then, I have work to do, projects to accomplish and a long list of tasks to complete.

Chapter Twenty

Rio Verde

The River Styx

Its been ten days and I really haven't left the bed except to throw up and do bathroom business. Every time I move my head I have extreme pain followed by a nausea that mostly leads to dry heaving until my throat nearly rips out. I've lost fifteen pounds and experience severe hot flashes from the Lupron every hour or so. It feels as if I've been in a car wreck because my body - bones and muscles – are alive with pain.

Passing through the bathroom I glance at myself and wonder who the pathetic wretch with the vacant eyes is looking back at me. I have bloody cold sores on my lips, in my mouth, around my nostrils and open bloody sores in my nose and sinuses. Blowing my nose, the tissue is filled with bloody scabs and mucus. When I wipe my ass today, the toilet paper was red with scabs. Using a mirror I see my rectum is ringed in open sores.

Seeing myself reminds of a Hieronymus Bosch painting of the diseased, nearly dead and the abhorrent dead crossing the inky black river Styx to the great marsh of the afterworld in classic Greek mythology. I am now one of the active dying and my veins are filled with fire and burning coals. The chemo is killing the cancer and its host – me. My nerve endings are fried, burned away in the inferno that runs unchecked.

My lungs must be scorched because I can't inhale enough oxygen to take away the sense that I'm suffocating. The only place I feel I'm sucking enough air is when I sit up in a chair, but after a while that doesn't work either so I dash outside hoping to find relief, but it's 105 degrees and I nearly collapse before making it inside.

How can I escape myself? How can I rid myself of this despair?

The wildfire that is my body has created a boiling headache and if I could sign my unfinished last will and testament I would drown my nightmarish existence in the neighbor's swimming pool.

Lana rushes me to Copperwood Cancer center where an on-call physician examines me and checks my records. Apparently, a mistake was made and somehow – by accident or incompetence – I was injected with a toxic dose of chemo drugs constituting toxicity levels that easily could be fatal.

My Darling Lana,

Please forgive me. This is the hardest thing I've ever written. If I could stay with you I would. But it is time to say goodbye and to broadcast my essence out into the unknown where I might merge with my Mother and all those I have loved and lost. We both knew this day would come and I will miss you with all of my heart and all that I am. You are the love of my life.

Everything has a beginning, middle and an ending. It is my hope that this ending is part of a metamorphosis and a new beginning will dawn and that somewhere and somehow we will be together again and share the love that blossomed out of our youth and grew into a vast and beautiful garden.

I love and cherish you and together life has been magical and for me. You are that magic that spark, that source of inspiration and meaning I've searched for since losing you so long ago.

We both hoped for many years ahead, years of loving and sharing, but sadly this will not happen now. We are both strong and forward looking and I will keep my eye on the horizon, searching for your loving face and true heart.

Please forgive me for this – for the pain you will experience and the separation we must endure. I do this now with the hope that your heartache and recovery will end one day sooner, that the sun will shine and your special life force will bloom one day sooner with laughter and new love. I do this now to save you from witnessing the misery of my slow demise and hope that you will remember me as a man filled with life, promise and love for you.

Lana my love, you are a remarkable woman, strong, capable, intelligent and spirited. Your beautiful spirit and deep soulful strength are the hallmarks that will now serve you well with tender and loving acceptance in our separation.

Thank you for the tenderness and strength you've shown taking care of me in this, my time of greatest need. Wish I could have done the same for you.

First, Last, Always.

-Mark

CHAPTER TWENTY-ONE

RIO VERDE

It's a week later and I haven't heard back from Walsh, but I just received a call from John Sugg, executive editor in chief of Freedom Magazine.

"Mark, I've just talked to executives in LA and they want you to send Chapter Two to them now. Please format it..."

"They want what?" I interrupt. "My deadline for this chapter isn't for another two weeks . . . it's unfinished . . ."

"They want to see it now, it doesn't matter what your deadline is or that it is unfinished . . ."

"It matters to me!" I respond. "Why are you calling me? You are not my supervisor on this project."

"It doesn't matter, I've been told to have you send it!" John voice changes, he sounds angry and heavy handed.

Silence.

"Tell them I'll send it on deadline. It is not formatted

in a way that's readable. You know I write in segments. As is, it is unreadable."

"Send it as it is."

"I'll send it on the deadline."

John goes off now, ranting about sending it or suffering the consequences. He threatens to fire me.

"Look, John, you are not my boss… I work here at the pleasure of the church and if the powers that be want to fire me, they can do it anytime they please."

"You know this could be your job, right?"

"Fuck you, John. From the beginning, I negotiated workable deadlines. I was hired for my expertise and talent. I've lived up to my part on the agreed progress reports and due dates – and I'll meet my deadline as agreed – and they can live up to theirs. I'll send the chapter when it's finished."

Click. John is gone.

Since my conversation with Sugg I've heard nothing from him or Walch or anyone else from LA or Clearwater. No one has supplied me with the Hubbard quotes so I've left places clearly marked in the twenty-five-thousand-word chapter for their insertion, if they truly exist – which I strongly doubt.

JUNE 1, 2017

A certified letter just arrived from Bruce Thompson, the Freedom International Magazine and Scientology executive whose job description might be listed as "overseer," informing me that my employment contract will terminated on the fifteenth of this month.

I can't say I didn't expect it – had they not fired me I would have quit on my own. There was no reason listed for my dismissal but I suspect the decision was precipitated by one of two situations. The first was my decision to exclude what the church considers significantly important historical material from Chapter Two for the book, Attacks on The Church of Scientology, because of the absence of evidence and verifiable documentation. I wasn't going to lie for them.

The second possible reason for my dismissal could be my refusal to submit my unfinished chapter weeks before its deadline. Sugg's demand occurred as I pressed church officials for the documentation needed to finish the book segment. I knew my outburst would not go over well, but I had proven my worth many times; and I was tired and sick and this incident fell at the end of a long line of unprofessional episodes and unfulfilled promises stretching back to the heady days of my hiring and the relaunch of Freedom

International Magazine.

HOLLYWOOD, CALIFORNIA

JANUARY 16, 2016

LOOKING BACK

The first editorial meeting of the newly reconstitut-ed Freedom International Magazine is about to get under way at the Scientology Media Center. The relaunch in-cludes a new staff of sixteen writers and editors. Ben Shaw, the church executive trouble-shooter and problem-solver based in Clearwater, worked for five years to make this project a reality. Rumor has it that billionaire and church member Robert Duggen gifted the church hundreds of millions of dollars and some of that money went to get Freedom off and running again. I suspect it wouldn't have happened at all without the gift.

"Okay, everyone find a seat," Shaw announces and the new staffers move from the coffee and donut table to long worktables assembled in a semi-circle.

I introduce myself to the man on my left, a longhaired fellow with an impressive mustache. He was about my age and wearing a heavy beat-up leather jacket.

"Mark Taylor," I say, extending my hand.

"Dan Luzadder," he replies, taking my hand. "Oh, nice

to meet you, too," he says. "John tells me you are good."

"Oh really, how nice of him," I answer surprised. "Too bad he's never told me that… Hope it pays off in salary negotiations."

Luzadder laughs.

Sugg, the new executive editor, has assembled an impressive staff. Included are three Pulitzer winners, top newspaper editors, seasoned news journalists and magazine feature investigative writers. None are Scientologists and the majority are here because of him. Sugg is a rotund Orson Wells type of southern gentleman who got his start as a red headed firebrand writer for the Miami Herald during and after the war in Vietnam. In an age before social media, Sugg was well respected and had a strong following. He was the executive editor of the alternative Creative Loafing brand of big city weeklies along the eastern seaboard. His work was crafty, smart and biting, taking on corporate executives, politicians and even major daily newspapers that ran afoul of journalistic canons.

Sugg's criticism of the St. Petersburg Times' (now the Tampa Bay News) coverage of the Church of Scientology became a celebrated battle in Florida pitting the newspaper titan against a freebie weekly. Sugg accused the powerful daily of lacking editorial integrity and his voice mimicked the church's claim of media bias and bullying.

On my other side is Aja Singh, a handsome middle-aged Indian whose first language is Hindi but speaks almost flawless English. He tells me he worked as an investigative writer for India Today, owned by Rupert Murdoch, until it was unceremoniously shuttered for not meeting financial goals.

"We were a real success," Singh says. "Doing great work and our circulation was in the millions. Murdoch pulled the plug anyway." He made a thumb's down gesture.

"Is that what brought you to the U.S.?"

"No, not really," he demurred and pointed with his forehead, "My wife is a professor here at Pepperdine."

"Well," Sugg starts with a big smile, "here we are for the first time. Look around," he pauses as we do the perfunctory one-eighty, "few writers get a ground floor opportunity like this; to be a part of new world-class media production company. It's taken more time and energy than it should have, but it's been well worth it. Ben here," he turns to Shaw sitting next to him, "even convinced me to leave my Georgia mountain top and move to this god-forsaken place (LA) to be a part of it."

A nervous laugh goes up.

"Our goal is to establish a world-class magazine, one

focusing on the major issues and problems facing the world today.

"You will have latitude to write about subjects in long form. We perceive pieces between 2000 and 5000 words and serialized pieces up to 10,000 words depending on the subject. Some of you, the most seasoned, will be able to generate your own story ideas and cover the material as you see fit."

"The church will take a back seat in the endeavor," Ben Shaw adds, "but of course, anything we publish will be attributed to the church so we need you to be sensitive to this.

"You have all been vetted and handpicked," Shaw says in a serious tone. "It's a dog-eat-dog world out there in the writing business. Thousands of journalists have been laid off and are searching for work, and the Internet is paying nothing. You can't even give your work away."

I glance around and most of my colleagues have their heads down clearly understanding his intent and feeling fortunate for this high paying job. Had the newspaper industry not collapsed, I doubt Freedom International would have been able to enlist such an accomplished staff.

Shaw made his point clear and goes on, "You will be working with a world-class design department here at SMP

(Scientology Media Productions) and our printing facility is one of the most modern and high tech anywhere in the country. We will be taking a tour of the facility later today."

"Really, the sky is the limit," Sugg says, smiling. "We will be publishing every month so we need you to go to work and get some excellent stories ready.

"If you want to write features or do investigations you can do that. If you want to try documentaries or multi-media presentations, we have the best equipped visual, audio and television facilities anywhere right on the property. If you are interested in writing books we plan to publish books in the near future."

For the next two days we toured the expansive Scientology facilities from its print division and special projects buildings, to the newly renovated historical film studio media center. Even for the most hard-bitten news editors, it's hard not to be impressed by the Scientology Media Center.

Freedom International Magazine got its start in 1968 as a pet project of founder L. Ron Hubbard, but in the years after his death it struggled and had been in an on-again off-again status for the last few years. The church had long wanted a megaphone to respond to critics and spread the news of good work of the church.

After years of hiatus, the Hollywood faction of the

church tried again to put the wheels back on the magazine with little success. The church was at war with the national media community and few writers or editors wanted to take a chance with them. On the other hand, the Florida faction, known as more pragmatic and the ecclesiastical and spiritual center of the church, got the nod to have a go at the magazine. Spearheaded by Ben Shaw with assistance from Sugg the two recruited a staff, moved to Hollywood and took charge.

But as months passed it became evident that none of the espoused goals were being implemented. I felt none of the essential esprit-de-corps for creating a winning and cohesive environment for success. After our initial editorial meeting we never met together again. There were no editorial schedules or matrices of stories being generated or scheduled for publication. Most writers had no idea what other writers and editors were doing. Worst of all, the monthly magazine issues were not being released in a timely fashion.

In one case I was told a new issue of Freedom was at the printer and weeks later when it didn't materialize and nothing was uploaded onto the website, I learned that church leader David Miscavige had taken issue with one of the stories and nixed the entire effort.

When I visited the LA offices they were always empty. The usual cacophony of activity created by news people rushing from one place to another, desperately trying to work amid the busy atmosphere was absent. No one except Sugg and a Scientologist editor, Gail Armstrong, had a designated office with their name on it.

Instead of a vibrant workspace, there was an eerie sense that something was wrong. I noticed Freedom's encrypted email portal, Proton mail, was programmed to hide all other staffers' email addresses. There was no networking and lists of writers' email addresses and telephone numbers were never issued. I was okay with this arrangement because I was working from my studio in Arizona, my paycheck was arriving on time, and I wanted nothing to do with office politics. When I asked Sugg why the magazines were not being released in a timely manner, he snapped, "There have been unforeseen delays. Don't ask again."

Okay, John.

Sugg, who was once outgoing and funny, turned angry and answered questions with one word replies. Most of the time he was not available to take calls. I have been in the editor's hot seat before and concluded he was stressed beyond his ability and doing the best he could just to survive. When I flew to the offices for meetings with my unqualified book editor, lawyer Bill Walsh, Sugg greeted me from his office doorway and then disappeared inside and locked the door.

Another time, he and Ben Shaw disappeared for several weeks and Joe Taglier, a talented young investigative writer, sent out a general distress email asking where John was and why he had gone missing.

Later, I learned that everyone was as mystified as I was. No one had any insight or answers. And this mystification quickly turned to anger when the few issues that were released were packed with articles that had little or no resemblance to those submitted by the authors. After spending months laboring over first class investigative pieces, they were so poorly edited the result was unreadable. Writers left in disgust.

My experience was a mixed bag. I spent four months generating a three-part series on capital punishment of the mentally ill and how jails and prisons had become America's new mental institutions. When the series was submitted, Sugg and Shaw raved and said they were scheduled as cover stories in upcoming issues, but they never appeared. When I enquired about the delay, Sugg said the stories were scheduled for later that year. To date, they have never been published.

By the end of the first fifteen months, all but three of the original staff writers were gone. Some quit and others were fired. Sugg and Shaw disappeared back to Florida. I was one of the three who remained but only because I was tapped to author a book for the church. Church leader David Miscavige was personally overseeing my progress.

In the final analysis, the grand experiment to establish a world-class investigative magazine and media empire failed – miserably. In my opinion, the entire enterprise was designed to fail from the beginning. I learned later that one faction of church executives was against the magazine from the start. They were unhappy with non-Scientologists working for the church and intentionally made changes and edits to stories rendering them unreadable.

Chapter Twenty-Two

Rio Verde

Round Table Three

One source of comfort in my effort to remain positive and relevant is my studio. It's a large open boxy space with fifteen foot ceilings, massive north and west facing windows looking out into the desert. The floor is a south-western style tile giving it a clean artistic appearance and the wall space is covered with original oil paintings and photographic art, including framed book and magazine covers representing professional milestones. Among these are scores of photographs chronicling my life reaching back to the early days of the 1970s.

If there is to be no future for me, I can still find solace in my past and the people, events and meaningful experiences my life represents. I often find myself standing in front of one piece of art or another hoping it might spark a clear light recollection hidden within or ignite some long-lost intimate detail that might burn inside me for a moment or two.

Invariably, I pause at a 1973 group photograph of the Lake Street Sluggers softball team. It is a large photograph, maybe 18 by 24 inches, and it's hard for me not to smile at this ragtag assemblage of undeveloped talent and potential. I see so much life yet to be lived, so many challenges to mount, so many promises to be made and broken, and so many defeats to overcome.

Looking at each person's face I can almost hear their voice. Time has passed and the black and white reproduction is dark around the outer edges, but the two rows of ball players at its center is still sharp and telling. We are posed after a game and one row is taking a knee and the other is standing behind it. On the bottom from left to right are Chris Berger, Vaughn Fuelner, Brad Holmquist, Scottie Wright, Larry Lewis and Ron Godfrey. Those standing behind include me, Bud Mixon, Mickey Tripp, Kelly Hoskins, Robin Johnson and Mike McPheron.

We are young and despite the long hair and half developed beards, we are handsome and filled with the excitement that only happens in youth when the world is a mystery and we have no idea what might to happen next.

I hear something behind me, then a voice.

"Why do you always stop and look at this one?"

"Nancy!" I wheel around excitedly, "It's you! You are here. Perfect!"

Standing next to me now, she is wearing the same beautiful white summer dress she wore the last time we were at the theatre together. She is thin and fragile, yet radiant. She flashes me a big happy smile – one I've longed to see.

"I guess it reminds me of good times," I answer.

"Don't you enjoy my oils?" She scans the room and spots one of her original oils.

"Of course I do, Nancy. I love them. But my favorite of yours is the Havana or Bust piece over here."

The original oil hangs nearby and portrays a male anti-war activist with long hair and a beard wearing a jacket with a tee shirt underneath that reads, "Havana or Bust." In his left hand he is pointing a revolver out at the viewer and in his mirrored aviator sunglasses are two images of Nancy facing him. Her long black hair is full and she is wearing a very low-cut red blouse.

"I've always loved that sexy self portrait of you!"

"Ha!" she laughs and slaps my shoulder. "I'm so glad you got that piece. It was meant to be yours."

She steps forward and takes a close look at each of

the Sluggers, "I was there that day," she recalls, "the day the photo was taken. "Remember? I was standing just outside the picture frame with Heather and Summer."

"Really? I'd forgotten."

"I was there with Patty Gillen and Norma Mannos," she goes on, swaying as if moving to music. "We brought the kids, too - three girls with four babies. It was tough, but we knew how to have fun. I remember being overwhelmed - school, the girls, money, being alone. If it weren't for friends, none of us would have made it."

A serious look washes over her face, followed by a wistful smile. "Such a long time ago... We were so young... those were the days," her voice trails off.

After a short silence, Mick pipes up, "Looks like you're up next, Taylor." He is standing behind Nancy and pointing at the photograph. He is wearing the rich pile ski sweater and tan trousers he wore in his coffin. "You notice you are the last one standing on the back row?"

"I've noticed, Mick," I catch his gaze and he mine.

"Bud's gone. Kelly's gone. Rockin' Robin's gone now. And Horse is gone, too. Of course I was the first... It was the first and only time I was first at anything... Down the big shit tube... the giant sucking sound, you know..." Shuffling his feet in a dance, he goes on, "All gone. Taylor. You are the last man standing."

"Eat me." I answer.

"Of course, he is," Nancy adds. "He is the last because he is our chronicler. Who will tell the stories? Where would we be without him? Who will tell our stories and keep us alive? I would have given anything to have lived longer – to have more time. Anything!

"Mark is sending messages from us to those we love and who love us still." She goes on, "Giving us life – breathing air into us. He is the magic sending messages to our loved ones."

"Anybody got any smokes?" Mick changes the subject, holding back laughter. "I'd give my left nut for a fucking derm about now. . . Alive!" he says scornfully. "Who the fuck gives a shit about being alive?"

"I care, Mick, and so do you," Nancy says softly. "I loved my life, every day of it. I, for one, left too early. I have grandchildren I've never met. I want my girls to always know who I was and to never forget me."

From behind my desk, another voice chimes in, "Time is not what you think, Nancy," It is Randall Potts, his voice is deep, smooth and soothing. He is surveying my papers. "Dying is not the end of everything. What happens on earth is only the beginning and whether looking back,

THE CAPITAL OF PARADISE: A MEMOIR

embracing the present, or searching for a future, it has all just begun."

"Randall!" I shout, "So glad you joined us!"

"Easy for you to say," Mick adds in. "Obviously, we lived different lives, my friend." He contorts his features into a grotesque face and making his hand into the shape of a gun, he lifts it to his temple, "Boom, mother fucker. . . Everyone is better off with me gone."

Nancy groans softly. Randall is placid and his face shows no emotion.

"You have suffered, Mick, I am so sorry," Nancy tries to comfort him, "but now you are saved and your spirit and soul can move toward the everlasting light. You may not know it, but you are here because of the afterlife you've earned. You were a good man, Mick, a troubled man, but honest, true and loved."

"I lived ethically because it offered a bit of stability and I was pragmatic," Mick conceded. "But I did none of those things – I had none of the qualities you speak of! Life was meaningless and endlessly boring. I spent unimaginable amounts of time feeling crazy and hating myself – self-loathing, yes, and jealousy, too. The anxiety and paranoia… I plotted killing people before they killed me…"

Mick lowers his head and begins to sob while Nancy,

Randall and I stand facing him. He continues, "My psychiatrist told me I was a genius and when I told Taylor about it, you know what he said to me? He said and I quote, 'Well, it might be true but I haven't seen any sign of genius in you as yet.' Can you believe it?"

A hearty laughter rings up and out among us and we all rock back with belly laughs. When the laughing momentarily subsides, we start laughing again and it grows and becomes contagious. We laugh and giggle until it morphs into grunts and postures and I can hardly stand or breathe; but here I am again with my beloved companions! Together once again… and I'm in heaven.

Mick laughs so hard he starts to cry and we all cry. It was one of those timeless moments of life and glory. He leaned over bracing his hands on his knees so as not to fall over. Nancy's face is flush red and she is clearly delighted and embarrassed, putting the back of her hand against her lips and nose. Randall stands as a sentinel might, blithely trying to be impassive, but unable to stop the herky jerky motions of his true elation.

"Thanks, Mick. We needed that," I say when I'm able to speak again.

Randall picks up a ballpoint pen sitting on my desk. It is emblazoned with The Beatles logo and he takes a closer look.

"Nice," he says. Looking directly at me and then at the others he changes the subject, "But we are not here for this, we are here to help you, my friend."

Suddenly, I am overcome by emotion, it fills my chest cavity and rushes up my throat and I can't breathe. Fearing I might collapse, I steady myself by holding the back of a nearby chair.

"Oh, Mark we love you!" Nancy says, comforting me.

Mick breaks down and cries again, but this time the tears are those of sorrow. He doubles over, holding himself, then sits on the tiled floor.

Regaining my composure, I try to speak, "I'm so sorry. Please forgive me. I'm just not myself anymore. I am not the person you remember."

"Yes! You are, too!" Nancy disagrees. "You are the strongest person I've ever known."

Shaking my head back and forth, "No, no, Nanc, No. I am not. The cancer and chemo have destroyed me. I am nothing but an empty shell. I can't find a way out." Breathing in and out deeply I repeat, "What do I do? What do I do?"

From the floor, Mick hides his face in his hands and sobs. Rocking back and forth, he says, "You know what you need to do, Taylor. It's time. Take yourself out! You're already dead... Who needs this life anyway?"

"No!" Nancy demands. "Every day is a gift, even the hardest days. It is not for you to decide," she says looking into my eyes. "Your time will come; let faith and your belief in all that is sacred take you when nature says the time is right. You must fight and never lose hope."

Mick howls and wipes tears away with the palms of his hands. He rests on the tile floor.

"I remember once at the Terrace Ballroom," Randall starts, "three guys were bullying a little guy and you felt the injustice and hollered at them to stop, but when they didn't you waded in and fought all three. Seconds later, it was over."

"Yes!" Nancy shouts. "That's right Marcus! You've never given up, see this to the end . . . you can do this . . . "

"But Nancy, I am not strong. That was long ago, this is different. "

"That's true, Mark," Randall says. "But I was not talking about your physical strength, I was referring to the strength of your convictions, spirit and character."

Randall struggles to continue, "At one time or another you saved each one of us. You were there when we needed you. We counted on you; your devotion to us . . .

Perhaps you've forgotten, but you carried each one of us to our graves. To our Earthly resting place."

"God damn you, Taylor!" Mick cries out.

Nancy lowers her head and sobs.

"You will know what to do when this time of deliberation is complete," Randall says with authority. "Trust yourself. You will know."

We are all quiet for some time.

"Well," I finally say, transfixed by the photo of the long-ago Sluggers, "At least I know now there is life – or something – after death."

Silence

"Right?"

Silence.

"Life after death… right?"

Turning to Randall, he disappears right before my eyes. Reeling around, Nancy and Mick are gone.

Looking around the room I see tears on the tiled floor where Mick sat crying. Bending down I want to touch one of the tears – to make sure it's real – but as I lean over another tear splashes down next to those already there.

CHAPTER TWENTY-THREE

ON THE ROAD

The road from Scottsdale to Flagstaff on I-17 is never easy and this morning the traffic crazies are out in masse. My heart pounds in my hands as they grasp the wheel. I hate this stretch of highway and try to avoid it unless it's absolutely necessary. The one hundred miles traverses up and down one mountain grade after another and offers beautiful contrasting Arizona views. My strategy is always the same, stay in the slow lane until forced to pass the slower truck traffic.

The highway caters to the five million people who live in the Phoenix basin and is a fusion of fast driving business and service vehicles, countless distracted tourists on their way to trendy Sedona or the Grand Canyon and thousands of large slow moving trailers, motor homes, and freight trucks crawling over steep mountain passes at walking speeds. The opportunity for deadly encounters is poised at nearly every milepost. I-17 could be the most dangerous well-designed highway in the country.

In the first sixty miles I pass four single car roll-overs – all European luxury SUVs – three bumper-to-bumper traffic jams and thousands of impatient motorists hell-bent on risking everyone's life to move up the grade faster than anyone else. The posted speed limit is 75 mph, but actual speeds exceed 85 to 90 miles per hour. For those like me who long to be on the road to relax and enjoy the world-class scenery and have a safe and sweet driving experience, this highway is not for us.

Luckily, it all ends in Flagstaff and most traffic goes either east or west on Interstate 40. After gassing up, I head north on Highway 89 across Navajoland.

After everything I've experienced recently and the perilous deleted future I face, I've decided to hit the road and retrace my footsteps across the land and back in time. For the last forty years I've explored northern Arizona and Southern Utah searching for the missing parts to the puzzle of my soul and the lost and buried archaeological treasures we leave behind. I've written four books about this land and its impact on us. It is my home.

It would be incorrect to say I am looking for answers. A more accurate assessment is I'm in need of the solace of these open and wild places. I've had a rich, meaningful and busy personal and professional life but I'm home among the silence, the wind and the lost sandstone canyons and towering escarpments. This land is my cathedral – the mysterious source of equanimity.

The road north of Flagstaff is lonely and quiet and has a serenity that nurtures me. The tight ball of my internal organs relaxes inside my abdominal cavity and my eyes seem to see further than the distant horizon. I have left the reckless turmoil that modern life engenders, and now I exist only in moments and thoughts and fleeting sights I experience.

Thirty miles passed the historic Cameron Indian Trading Post, I take the famed Navaho Trail northeast toward Tuba City and Kayenta. The afternoon sun is sinking and the Painted Desert comes alive in pink, red, blue and aquamarine pastels. The hills roll over themselves and create one silhouette nestled atop another, each a different shade of pink, blue and purple. A few miles further I pass the turn off for Moenkopi and Hotevilla. It reminds me of the first time I visited Hopiland. At the time I was low on gas and stopped at Hotevilla, but there was no exit, just scores of double track tire trails leading to some low buildings a short distance away. I was traveling with my big boy, Bask – The Lionhearted. Bask was a huge and beautiful Doberman Pinscher. When I stopped to ask directions from some black-haired Hopi boys who were playing on the hardened ground near the roadway, they approached with eyes wide open.

The boys couldn't take their eyes from the majestic Bask standing in the back seat.

"Is he brave?" one boy inquires in a most formal voice.

"Yes," I answer mimicking his tone. "He is brave." Another asks, "Would he fight a mountain lion?"

I considered the question for a moment before responding, "Yes, if the mountain lion was going to attack me, he would fight."

With that, they laughed, smiled and concurred, "He is brave."

Further on I pass the exit for Tuba city and remember in the old days there was no exit for Tuba City, the main road highway 163 ran straight down Main Street. Twenty-five miles further I enter Kayenta and decide to get gas and tour the thriving Navajo community. Before entering the business district, I pass the old Stop & Shop, a convenience store I often frequented when I needed a pay phone and to buy beer and supplies. It has been closed for a long time now and its shadowy hulk sits in the dark, the days of its usefulness long gone.

The Stop & Shop is where I met Brigham Joseph Atene, my beloved Navajo friend, one-time guide and traveling companion. I remember well the night we met. Brigham Joseph Atene saved my life that night.

Kayenta is one of those places where an uncertain dominant society finds itself the landlord of land occupied by a proud and reluctant subordinate society. There is much anger over what Anglo society has done to the Dineh culture and society. The American and the Native American cultures meet and comingle here for the sake of commerce, yet a palpable sense of tension hangs in the air.

On the night we met, I had just spent several days camping out on Hopiland and arrived in Kayenta itching for a cold Coke and needing a telephone to report to my editor in New York. It was during one of these calls that Brigham and I met. I will never forget that night.

"Spare change?" A deep voice asks from the sidewalk behind me.

Turning I find a buffalo-sized Navajo man, Brigham Joseph Atene, standing before me. He is wearing and oversized army-style camouflage jacket that pulls to accommodate his tremendous shoulders and fifty-gallon girth. An alcohol-induced stupor deadens his eyes.

"Yutahey," he says slowly. Brigham is unsteady and wavers like a great tree in the wind.

I retrieve the contents of my front pocket and drop it into his grizzly-bear-sized hand. Along with some quarters, dimes and nickels are several gum wrappers and pieces of wadded-up wastepaper. Brigham patiently picks out the trash from the coins and drops it to the ground. A garbage can is five feet away. When he is finished, he turns and walks away without saying a word.

A few minutes later a shadow casts down over me. He is back.

"Spare change?" He is now standing at attention, like a military man. "Yutahey," he says in a clear and resonant voice.

"I gave you all my change," I tell him.

"Not enough."

"For what?"

"Mad Dog." He stares at his open hand as if it will tell the story. The coins lying there look like miniature counterfeits.

"No more change," I answer resolutely.

"Spare change?" he repeats again.

Suddenly, I feel anxious. I am an alien on foreign soil. Navajoland is a sovereign nation. I am a visitor here. My energy may not be wanted. My American-ness may not be appreciated.

"Look," Brigham says in perfect English, "I am drunk. I will be sober tomorrow. I have come from San Francisco. I am alone." His huge chest rises and falls with sadness.

"You don't live here?" I ask.

"It was my home long ago. I am here because my grandmother is dying," he pauses as if trying to control his emotion. "I will go to her place tomorrow. Tonight, I am afraid to go home." He pulls the long greasy hair away from his face and looks down at me.

I am speechless.

"I will get sober tomorrow," he says again. "Help me buy some hooch. I will share it with you."

"Thanks," I say, "but no thanks. I'm waiting for someone." Pulling my wallet from my back pocket, I ask, "How much for a bottle of Mad Dog?"

"I knew you was a good man!" he says relieved. He then reaches out to grasp my shoulder in a gesture of goodwill, but instead loses his balance and falls on me. For several moments we dance around in a circle, struggling to stay afoot. He smells of bitter layers of sweat, alcohol and motor oil.

Brigham disappears into the store and when he reappears he is carrying a brown paper bag pushed against his midsection like a fullback protecting a football. Turning to me he raises the bottle over his head, hollers something and disappears around the corner.

A few minutes later he is back again. He circled around the back of the building and is standing at its corner. He nods to me.

"What?" I ask impatiently.

"Over here."

"You come over here," I answer.

He makes a few tentative steps forward; he is accustomed to doing what white men tell him. Nodding to the bottle in his hand and then to the street, he says, "Federales."

For the very first time Brigham really sees me. "You a Vietnam vet?" he asks, spraying me with wine and spit.

"Aren't we all?" I snap a sharp salute.

He lifted the bottle out and away from his body, arcing it in a circle. "We are all veterans of this Vietnam, and of this heartless motherfucking world!"

He stands at attention and salutes me. "Corporal Brigham Joseph Atene. Reporting for duty, sir."

"At ease, soldier," I say. Something occurs to me. Once I had seen Atene's silhouette, his torso, chest, and face chiseled in a sandstone cliff. It was far out in the wilderness and I had forgotten all about it.

"Eighty-second Airborne. Two tours in Nam. The Ashau Valley." He salutes again, this time with the bottle to his lips. He holds the bottle out and I grasp it. I put it to my lips and take several long pulls.

"Holy sweet mother of pearl!"

"We can't talk here," Atene mumbles, taking the bottle quickly away from me. "Around back."

Behind the store, four young Navajos are sitting on the hardened, oil-soaked ground. Thousands of sharp pieces of green, brown and clear glass from broken wine bottles surround them.

Atene and I sit on a mound of dirt and talk. Night falls and the occasional errant headlights of a car out on the highway catch the shards of glass and transform them into sparkling jewels.

"I took the scalps of some gooks," Brigham tells me, "and it made me go crazy. The doctors said it was battle fatigue or Agent Orange, but I took the spirits from these men and I've been paying for it ever since."

One of the young men nearby approaches and takes the bottle from Brigham and drinks from it. He then performs a flawless Michael Jackson moonwalk across the carpet of glass to his friends who are waiting at attention. They help themselves until the bottle is finished off.

I give Corporal Brigham Joseph Atene enough money for two more bottles and when he returns he continues telling his story. Brigham was raised outside of Window Rock where his father had been a uranium miner until he fell sick and died. When the family finally learned he died of radiation poisoning, there was nothing they could do.

"He wasted away in our hogan," Brigham said. "He was a true patriot, but he was never accepted by the country he gave his life to protect."

Atene breaks down and cries. He covers his face and rocks back and forth, then side to side. His pain is hard to watch. I want to put my arm around him to give him comfort, but I dare not.

After awhile, he goes on with his story. He says that not long after his father died, his mother died, too, and he and his sisters were sent off to the Indian School in Brigham City, Utah. His sisters married Mormons and he was drafted into the army. Once in the army he learned about drugs and alcohol. When he returned from Vietnam his sisters denied him; their new lives did not include room for a drunk. Since then Brigham lived in exile, separated from his family and from the country that betrayed him.

He is back on the reservation now for the first time in years because his grandmother is very ill.

The four young Navajo join us. We pass the third bottle of Mad Dog around and Atene continues his story. Just as he was telling us about his Uncle Larry, who was a code talker in WWII – a name given to Navajo who befuddled the Japanese radio transmission code breakers by speaking Navajo – and who had been killed by stepping on a land mine shortly after the end of the war, one of the young Navajo pipes up.

"Why do your people take everything from us?" He is staring at me. His friends join in with magnificent war whoops.

"Your people killed our ancestors, stole our land, and now keep us out here. There is nothing out here! Nothing!" His voice is high-pitched, nasal and shrill. "You kill our fathers, you take our sisters, and you turn our brother into this!" He points to Atene.

"He did nothing to you!" Atene shouts.

Unable to contain his anger any longer, the young brave jumps to his feet and throws the nearly empty bottle of fortified wine against the back wall of the building. Boom! Glass and wine rain down over us.

"You think you can assimilate us – but you can't!" He

reaches down and grasps a piece of broken glass. "We do not want you here. No one gave you permission to come onto our land!"

Atene stands, "He is with me!"

Realizing the situation is fast getting ugly, I get to my feet.

"You have taken everything from us, but you cannot take my life – only I can do that!" Extending his arm, he draws the piece of glass down along the soft skin of the inside of his arm. His friends are staggering around, screaming incoherently.

"You can try to save me, but it is no use. I am as good as dead!"

I did not move to save him. The thought never entered my mind.

He extends his arm out to show us his blood, but surprisingly there is none. His friends take a closer look. An expression of shock comes over his face and his friends cry out to the heavens.

"Sit down and shut up!" Atene orders.

"We will drink ourselves to death then," the brave says. "We are The People!"

Suddenly, the young brave rushes forward toward me, but before I can move to protect myself, Atene – the ex-United States Army Ranger – stands between us and absorbs his tribesman's anger.

"Go! Quickly!" Brigham tells me. "Go, my friend of Nam."

Sometime later Brigham Joseph Atene got sober and became a respected elder of his clan. He is now the man he would have been had our Anglo society not intervened. Years later, he told me, "I took the long way home."

After staying the night in Kayenta, I was back on the road early headed toward Mexican Hat and Cedar Mesa. About forty miles outside of town, as I climb a rounded ridge covered in sage and dead snake grass I see a turn off and a small sign to the right and sense that it might be important. Slowing down, the letters emerge: Big Mountain 25 miles.

I pull to the side of the road down a sandy turn around and park. Big Mountain. It played a big part in my life back in the 1980s. Getting out of the car I stretch and consider taking a ride to Big Mountain and back in time. Last time I was there I swore I'd never return.

Big Mountain and The Sun Dance

"You asleep?" Crow Dog asks, poking his head into my tent.

"What?" I respond, half awake. "Who could sleep..."

Crow Dog drops the tent flap and walks away. As he goes, he warns me, "Keep a low profile, the hotheads don't like you – any of the Anglo."

"As if I didn't know that by now," I mutter to myself. I intend to stay right where I am. What have you gotten yourself into, Mark, I ask myself.

Associated Press writer Lori Wienrob pushes into my tent next, collapsing on a hip and elbow.

"We've got to get out of here." she begs, voice warbling.

"I don't know... I hadn't thought of..."

"Someone's going to get hurt," she interrupts. "I can just feel it."

About the same time, Anselm, a famous German photographer and his assistant/girlfriend Salka push into the dome tent. We sit Indian style. Head lowered, Anselm mutters, "I don't know man, I feel like I've been here before. I don't like it. Something is not right. I've covered war zones and not felt this kind of visceral hostility."

No matter that Russell Means and the steering committee of AIM (the American Indian Movement) invited us – a half dozen journalists and photographers – to chronicle the ceremony, they are not here and the rank and file braves want us gone. We are poison – the personification of what they fought against for the last 150 years. The previous night's collective craziness and violence terrified us.

Salka cries, "I had to pee and snuck out into the trees, but I was followed by this deranged looking native guy wearing war paint. He followed me, watching from behind some bushes. He gave me a most hateful look. He has this huge knife on his belt and when he saw me watching, he smiled and ran a finger across his throat and made a cutting sound!"

Salka does not look well and I thought she might be having a breakdown.

Last night's ceremonial powwow for today's Sun Dance ramped up until it was out of control. Many braves drank whiskey and were itching to fight. Hatred toward whites – even those trying to chronicle events – nearly boiled over. More than 200 young raving Native American braves danced to drums, smoked ceremonial pipes and competed with other tribes for attention by bellowing out their most blood curdling war cries. They danced in a huge circle and represented more than forty tribes - the Sioux, Cheyenne, Apache, Shoshone, Blackfoot, Crow and Navajo. They came to fight the Arizona National Guard and each brave carried within them the historic crimes against his tribesmen at the hands of white Americans. They were looking to settle the score. It was time to stand and fight!

The Sun Dance is the most powerful and mysterious of all Native American religious ceremonies. Non-natives – meaning white men – were barred from witnessing the dance generations ago. The dance is the product of religious visions, hallucinations and premonition dreams. Each represents sacrifice, kinship and brotherhood. The ceremony requires the braves to bare their chests and have a long sharpened deer or antelope antler pierce their breast. The long antlers enter one side of the breast and exit out the other side. The antlers protrude from the breast on both sides. It is a bloody and wildly painful procedure. Some braves cry out in pain, others pass out and drop to the ground. After the antlers are inserted, rawhide thongs are attached to the antlers and the braves are lifted off the ground and suspended there. By submitting to this gruesome, painful and debilitating ceremony, the individual is sacrificing himself to the spirit strength of the tribe.

The night before the Sun Dance the braves danced around a huge bonfire and whipped themselves into a frenzy. Shadows cast out onto the trees and rocks created a ghostly and nightmarish scene. Many paraded in front of Anselm so he could take their photograph. Some pulled knives and pretended to taunt and mock attack us. Others fired high power rifles into the sky or practiced war hoops and dance moves. One exceptionally drunk brave cursed me and spit at me. When I spit back – a huge mistake – he lunged toward me, but was restrained by the crowd. He swore he would kill me.

Thankfully about eleven o'clock in the morning a line of trucks arrived and the crowd went wild, running to greet the newcomers with war hoops and cheers. For the first time in hours, the pressure cooker was neutralized. We felt relieved, but worried too. Crow Dog, who brought us to the Sun Dance ceremony, said Russell Means had arrived and was going to speak. He told us sit at the edge of the large dirt flat area.

"Whatever you do, don't take pictures or use flash bulbs!"

"Right," I responded.

After Means spoke, mostly in Sioux, the dancing, drumming and war cries continued with renewed intensity.

I was covering the story as a freelance feature writer on assignment for the Salt Lake Tribune and Utah Holiday Magazine. After years of contentious negotiations, the Hopi/Navajo Land Redistribution Act had arrived at a pivotal moment. The Navajo, who lived on Big Mountain, had been ordered to relocate as part of the final agreement, but they refused to leave. When one deadline after another came and went, the BIA (Bureau of Indian Affairs) ramped up efforts and threatened forced evictions leading to the current confrontation.

It was decided during our morning tent discussion that I should talk to Crow Dog about leaving as soon as possible. After an unsuccessful search, I sat at the edge of the rocky outcropping and watched as another line of trucks and cars snaked up the grade into the meadow.

By noon a hundred additional armed braves arrived with more coming every hour. At the same time, organizers monitoring a radio station out of Flagstaff heard that Arizona governor Bruce Babbitt was considering mobilizing the Highway Patrol and State Guard to uphold the law and arrest anyone interfering with the Big Mountain/BIA deadline and evictions. Tensions ran high.

From my vantage point I watched as the leadership council huddled next to the Sun Dance tree. They talked and argued and used topographical maps to study the area. Arms were outstretched this way, then that way, gesturing toward high points along the ridge above the dirt road. They were planning to defend their position. A wave of fear swept over me. We might be stuck here and could become hostages or bargaining chips if violence brakes out. I left and searched for Crow Dog again.

I find him at his truck with his head under the hood.

"Crow!" I called out.

"Yes, Mark."

"We need to get out of here!"

He slowly brought his head out smiling, "Not waiting for the Sun Dance?"

I said nothing and gave him a deadpan look.

"Yes, my friend, I agree. You need to leave now – while you can," he went on. "It is not safe for Anglos."

Dog thought it best to leave without goodbyes or attention. He would figure it out and get back to me.

By early afternoon the mood changed. A solemn and slow dance moved counter-clockwise around last night's bonfire while others began gathering at the Sun Dance tree. At the tree, a revered Navajo medicine man wearing Levis, an old blue shirt and a red bandana around his long silvery hair chanted softly and pounded on a small drum.

From the crowd five or six young braves stepped forward and knelt in front of him with heads bowed. The Sun Dance ceremony had started. As the medicine man continued chanting and drumming, Crow Dog found me and raised his eyebrows. He gestured with palms down pushing toward the ground.

"Time to go. Get the others. Meet at my truck."

I nodded.

By the time we met Dog at his truck, one of the braves was being readied for the ceremony. Everyone's attention was on the sacred ceremony. From the bed of Dog's truck we could see the man's chest covered in blood and men securing the rawhide straps around the antlers. Using a motorized camera, Anselm snapped scores of photographs with a telephotographic lens.

Dog turned the key, but nothing happened. He tried again and again and with each attempt our hearts dropped. I jumped from the truck's bed and Dog and I opened the hood. "I was afraid of this," he groaned. "Dead battery or loose connection."

By this time the first brave had been lifted off the ground and into the Sun Dance tree. His chest was positioned upward and blood covered his bare torso. From our distance, it appeared he was unconscious. His arms hung to the sides and his head fell dangerously backward.

Dog and I frantically pounded on both cables to the battery and he quickly got inside the cab and tried again. Nothing. I grabbed one of the cables and turned it down hard, hoping for a better connection. Suddenly the engine started, I dropped the hood and jumped back into the bed of the truck. As we drove away we watched the second brave being hoisted into the air. He cried out in pain and struggled back and forth. It was difficult to watch. No one saw us leave or I believe cared that we were gone.

I decide against disturbing my recollections of the mountain and what happened there so long ago so I return to the car and leave. I read somewhere that the Sun Dance location was turned into a tribal camp area and the Sun Dance tree still stands in the middle of a flower covered meadow, a testament to the ongoing and long festering relationship between a proud and defeated culture and one that has never acknowledged responsibility for the holocaust it created.

CEDAR MESA AND BEARS EARS, UTAH

The graded dirt road to the top of Cedar Mesa winds back and forth up a treacherous grade more than fifteen hundred feet. From the top, the views looking south across the Valley of the Gods and into Monument Valley are spectacular and otherworldly. The expanse of high desert plains is populated by some of the most dramatic monoliths on planet Earth. These vistas stretch southward more than one hundred miles. Standing alone in this vast expanse are The Three Sisters, The Eye of the Sun, El Capitan and Totem Pole. These massive sentinels cut deep into the sky across a palate of blue, pink, gold and purple.

A few miles north on the cedar and juniper covered mesa, once home to a thousand generations of ancient Anasazi Indians, I find the secret entrance to a two track trail that disappears into the forest and canyons. I am home here having camped along this forgotten route many times over the decades. It has been the source of peace and tranquility throughout much of my life. I will stay put here in the tranquility and magic in an effort to understand all that has transpired until I decide to go.

After setting up camp I visit a nearby Anasazi burial mound I found many years ago. The site was desecrated by Navajos many generations ago searching for jewelry and other valuables. The human bones, broken pottery and discarded stone tools disturbed in the distant past still sit where I last viewed them. There are scores of mounds and campsites in the area and I sit on a dead and twisted cedar where I've lunched and contemplated in times past. By late afternoon, I have fallen into a deep contemplative loop. I learned early in life that trouble with work, family, relationships and life could easily be kept a bay in the commotion of the city, surrounded by the push and ferment of active life. But in the desert, the depth of life's circumstance cannot be disregarded. What is, *is*, and out here it finds a way into the light.

Meandering slowly through the forest, I spot a pottery shard and leaned down to examine it. Whatever it is, it's larger than I expected and most of it is buried in the red dirt. When I free the piece from its perennial resting place I discover it is an unbroken bowl with exquisite paint and design.

Later, I build a firepit, sit on an old twisted cedar trunk and lose myself in the deep red coals and dancing flames. I am at peace and this is where I belong tonight. Spreading a tarp out I lie atop my sleeping bag and watch the night sky and Milky Way. The mournful howl of coyotes comes to me from many directions and I drift away to this wild melody.

One of the deepest patterns within mankind is that of departure and return, so it seemed right that I left my camp in the predawn light and carefully picked my way to a cliff edge some distance away. Darkness is still in control as I work around ancient juniper trees, over expanses of rimrock that sound hollow under my feet and through deep gardens of bronze and orange sand. The Hopi call this time of day Nuptu, meaning dawn's purple light of creation. To the east, the cauldron of new light intensifies and wells up, spreading along the horizon and up into the starry sky. At this time of day, I feel in perfect tune to some immense vibrancy, to some pure essence of life.

I will work my way deep into the unknown wilderness on this day, venturing out past the blue horizon to places where silence and solitude mark each day unbroken. The land will pick my pathway, and I will honor its wisdom, going places only serendipity goes, for there is a special "returning to myself" waiting out there.

I arrive at the edge of the cliff just as the sun tips the eastern horizon and the new light rushes across the plateaus and monuments, pouring down into the canyons and valleys. In the swelling rhythm of new light and discovery, I am conducted to the edge of the world, to the uttermost frontier of tangible thought. Somewhere in the morning light, I think I glimpse the final passageway through the stone mountains and down into the valley far below. I do not stay long before making tracks south, following a line of rimrock until it plunges into the uncharted forest.

I will penetrate deep into the most inaccessible area of the plateau, hiking miles out and returning the next day.

Over the years I have made many mistakes out here and surely I will make more. And though I am less inclined to act before thinking, this powerful land still takes me where it would have me go.

I move slowly toward some unknown destination, drawn out onto the enormous mesa by some inexplicable force. Ridge after ridge, canyon after canyon all whisper my name and send me forward. Yet, long after my heart and soul have surrendered to this power, my well-ordered intellect continues to ruminate. My mind can't help but question all that I am feeling, for it has learned to protect me and is uncomfortable with such a powerful simplicity. Ultimately, my intellect concedes and admits that something indeed very special is taking place within me, something that soothes and nourishes like nothing else.

Destinations are irrelevant here; the search and the satisfaction of discovery along the way are what is important. Nonetheless, I will know my destination when I see it, though I've never been here before. A long hike lies ahead, but I am happy to proceed further and further into this torrid, chaotic expanse of boulders, spires, ridges, hogback domes, and endless sage and juniper-covered flats. The pathway opens up before me as I walk into it, and then closes behind me as if sealing me into its magic.

It has been thirty-years since my first visit to this plateau. Back then, I spent ten days alone here, and after a particularly difficult transition from the frenetic discontent of the city to the solace of these open spaces, I experienced a rarefied sense of peace and well-being. I felt what the lone wanderer, poet, and artist Everett Ruess once felt. Before his mysterious disappearance in 1934, Ruess wrote this passage to his brother:

I prefer the saddle to the streetcar and star-sprinkled sky to a roof, the obscure and difficult trail, leading into the unknown, to any paved highway, and the deep peace of the wild to the discontent bred by cities. Do you blame me for staying here, where I feel that I belong and am one with the world around me?

After chugging up a steep white dome, I discover a canyon system snaking off to the south. It was not on my topographical map, but this is not really that unusual. Over the years I have discovered hundreds of such canyons not represented on maps. What is unusual is that this land changes so suddenly and dramatically: from rolling hills to deep canyons, from towering cliffs to forested flats, from slanting ridges to barren shelves, from dry washes to mesas, from steep drainages to petrified sand dunes. This land evolves, morphs, and transforms. It repeats itself, beginning or ending something new; finishing or starting something old. It is unpredictable, yet predictable, different but the same, unique but uniform.

For several hours I move over a long rimrock-covered plateau; my body comes alive under the burden of the hike and the building heat of the day. The cancer and my treatments have weakened my body, but my spirit and determination are strong. My tendons and muscles stretch and contract like the rigging of a well-worn ship, and my arms and legs sweep back and forth like a gyroscope, keeping me in balance as I scan the territory before me - not so much gauging or mapping it, but seeing it for the first time, consuming its fresh vision.

I wonder if I might see others out here. Over the years, I have seen many satellite souls on this land. I suspect they are also searching for pieces of themselves. They may be rebelling against the obscene isolation of the city and have journeyed to the wild to find comfort in the isolation of nature. For me, this isolation, this silence, this beauty, and this immense emptiness and absence are necessary to shock me fully awake so I might have a greater sense of awareness that is impossible to acquire elsewhere.

Out here the expectations and judgments of man are hushed, as if they were swallowed up by the huge, vibrantly modulated walls of silent sandstone. This silence restores the kinship between the outside and the inside of me. This silence is soulful and seductive; it changes people – forever. The mystery inside us all is enlivened by the intense stillness. This mystery is not the psychological enigma of a Mona Lisa, but the mystery encountered when facing the sheer, massive physical presence of the natural world. For the earth is the prime repository and source of nature's inexhaustible and indivisible energy. The silence has density and fills the land to the brim, presenting us with a solid, yet penetrable front.

In the mid-morning heat, I cross a valley where the land is burned, cracked and scalded. It is covered with scars, boils, and blisters. It reminds me of my father's leathery back when he was an old man and working shirtless in the family vegetable garden. He worked hunched over in the summer sun and his tawny, tanned and leathery hide reflected light just as the sandstone does passing under my feet.

Moving into a new section, I encounter a valley populated with checkerboard domes of eroded Navajo sandstone the size and shape of the great pyramids at Giza.

Hugging the base of these monuments and growing high onto their shoals are tall, strong-looking ponderosa pines. The scene is real, but somehow unreal. I stop to take a long look. Perspectives and forms tilt forward, as if erected by the energy within them, pressing out against line and form. I see my mother sitting on the swirling sediments, but when I look again she is gone. There is nothing there.

During the middle part of the day the desert invites mistakes. Steamy vistas and evaporating horizons can draw a person out into dangerous situations. Newcomers should be cautious; the heat and harsh blinding light plays tricks on vision and depth perception so that distance and height cannot be trusted. At midday the land becomes ugly, inhospitable and especially unforgiving, yet it still possesses the power to pull even reserved, cautious individuals out onto it, as if offering the answer to some great mystery – perhaps destiny itself – that lies just over the next horizon.

At this unmerciful time of day, I usually try to stay inactive, making few decisions and never striking out into the unknown unless absolutely necessary. But this day is an exception and I hike through the heat, resting often and drinking plenty of fluids. I stop in the shade of a rock outcropping at the mouth of a secret canyon and lunch on raisins, cheese, crackers, and melted chocolate.

I sit in the intimacy of this lost box canyon where the rocks are so old I can crush them easily in my bare hands. They are pressed of tiny fossils and sand from an ancient ocean. I am face to face with the basic material, the raw and irreducible elements that make up the surfaces of Earth, Moon and Mars.

Everything speaks of eternity here, of vast amounts of time passing, of the immense power of the natural world. This could be the most powerful contemplative setting on Earth. For as far as the eye can see, everything remains as it was created, without human touch, mark, or intervention. For me, this lonely and wild land somehow reacquaints me with ideas of spirit, soul and of my own fragility.

At the bottom of some strung-out ridges, my path has a hypnotic effect and I am quite satisfied to watch it come and go as I wind my way into it. I have been at it for many hours, working my way through twists and turns, up and down hills, around deep canyons, through sagebrush flats, and across desolate plateaus where I could see a hundred miles in every direction.

From the highest places, I see the curvature of the earth. Years ago, this phenomenon troubled me. It was easy and natural for me to believe I was at the center of creation, the biggest guy on the block. But when confronted with this larger metric – Earth rolling through space – the significance of my insignificance humbled me.

Working through a pinion and juniper forest I realize there are actually two forests here, one that is alive and one that is dead. These two forests stand intermingled in the secret canyons, on the hillsides, and across the wide and varied plateau tops. It is difficult to tell which is which, the living from the dead; both are austere and both lift their boughs to the heavens, swirling and dancing like flames and inviting the muse in me to come to life. Many of these trees are centuries old and others have been dead for centuries. Walking among them it is easy to honor them as I honor architecture, battlefield and art. This wood invites the proud and obstinate part of me to rise up and rejoin the passion play of life. Despite my diagnosis and my eventual demise, like these two forests I will lift my arms and spirit up to the heavens and dance in life's flame.

By late afternoon the bone-white moon and the porous red-hot sun have crossed the blue heaven making the monuments and buttresses sundial through time, and casting shadows across great expanses of hills and minor canyons populating this place. This little-known territory is a secret garden of Homeric pursuit; a place where Cyclops and the Serene of Silence could breathe free and where lesser souls – like myself – are humbled by the vast, un-adorned grandeur.

Just before dusk I find my campsite hidden in a grove of cedar and juniper trees. I know this campsite well; never mind that I have never been here before. I sit at the edge of the grove near a cliff line, perched high above the rest of the world, and watch as the dusk settles in the cliff eddies, and the silver fairy dust mixes with the umber, vermillion, and oxide rust of the sandstone. At this time of day, the green of the high-desert forest turns black and the tops of the sagebrush colonies glow with blue as if by magic.

From my vantage point, the foreground drops away into shadows and silhouettes of hips and shoulders, bellies and buttocks. To the southwest, one hundred miles away, the crest of the sacred Navajo Mountain disappears into a vaporous pink. To the north, Bear Ears speaks of genera-tions of natives whose lives revolved around winter on the plateau where I camp and summer in the high country.

What a magnificent time to live! At times like this, it is impossible not to feel a tremendous sense of fulfillment and joy. Everything *is* as I've always wanted it to be. I am a minute, but integral part of all of this. I am not complete without it, and it is not complete without me.

The dominion of dusk is now firmly in control, yet

on a far-off plateau, maybe seventy-five miles away in Monument Valley, a castle of Navajo sandstone blazes like fire with the last rays of sunlight. The castle stands against the dusk, as if to say, "This moment is mine! Watch me burn." In the time it takes me to say goodbye to the life I have known, the castle transforms into the blades of many knives. The blades cut and tear into the new night, spilling out the purple haze.

CHAPTER TWENTY-FOUR

BATON ROUGE, LOUISIANA

MARCH 2020

TRANSFORMATION

The flight to Baton Rouge gave me the opportunity to consider the spiritual arc we traverse on our blustery ride through this life. Earlier in the day, I visited Dance at the Edge Retreat where she conducts enlightenment workshops. Dance is the name Dave Thomson gave to his sister Emme when she was a kid. The idea of enlightenment started me thinking about transformational experiences and how one must be prepared to leave part or all of our previous life behind to start a new one.

After leaving Dance, I was struck by the notion that she is probably more like Dave than anyone else in the family and how this could be the key to finding him. Dave and Dance possessed a rare and difficult to define connection – that weaving of genetic and cosmic threads that bind some family members together in a powerful psychic web. By extrapolating from Dance's current metaphysical path, I wonder if she could be a working template for what Dave might be doing now. In some inexplicable co-mingling of sibling destiny, Dance may be mimicking her older brother's lead, each using their special talents to reach people in a spiritual way.

If after Dave's departure he had a life-changing spiritual experience that placed him at a transformational crossroad, I suspect he would not have followed a conventional route, that of say a born again Christian or a member of a mainstream religion. My guess is Dave would have embraced a more esoteric path, perhaps becoming the leader of his own spiritual or philosophical movement - collected of disparate metaphysical parts.

For people starting over, whether reluctantly forced into it by circumstance, or those like Dave who have chosen it freely, the path of spiritual transformation offers some attractive and substantial built-in advantages. You can remain largely anonymous; no one questions your motives or what brought you there; you are embraced by others who already share your new beliefs; and, in many cases, you can drop into a ready-made community and support system. I know this because as an undercover investigative writer I've done it.

I am not alone. Take psychiatrist and ex-president of Serbia, Radovan Karadzic, for example. After sending armies into Bosnia and Croatia to ethnically cleanse thousands of innocent Croats and Bosniaks, and twice being indicted by the United Nations war crimes tribunal in The Hague for genocide, Karadzic simply vanished in plain sight. For more than ten years he was listed as the world's most wanted man, yet he walked openly among the crowds in Belgrade, the country's capital city.

Karadzic created a new identity by becoming a new-age counselor of alternative medicine and Christian Orthodox spirituality and meditation. He taught classes, participated in conferences, was interviewed on television, and had a small following. In 2004, he even published a book. He went unrecognized because he grew a beautiful white beard and let his hair grow to his shoulders, wearing it in a ponytail. To his neighbors, he was the bearded older guy with the piercing eyes.

Or how about Kathleen Ann Soliah, who in the 1970s was a member of the ultra-violent Symbionese Liberation Army (SLA), most famous for kidnapping publishing heiress, Patty Hearst? Soliah was involved in a Sacramento bank robbery where one bank patron, a mother of four, was shot dead. Shortly afterward she disappeared without a trace. The SLA went on to rob more banks and assassinate the superintendent of the Oakland, California school district before being tracked down to its hideout where a shootout killed the group's founder and five members.

Soliah resurfaced in Minnesota as Sara Jane Olson and married a doctor. For twenty-four years, Sara Jane was a well-known member of a local church and a community activist. She was a mother, housewife and part-time actress; she raised money for the poor and read to the blind. After being profiled on America's Most Wanted television show, she turned herself in and went to prison for her participation in the SLA crimes.

Dave was neither hiding from the authorities, nor had he committed a crime as far as anyone knows, but even when the authorities are actively pursuing someone, it is easy to go undetected and start over in a society that rewards religious, spiritual or even personal transformation.

While in Louisiana, I will visit the State Human Identification Laboratory to check the unidentified remains of a man whose description matches Dave's, and then onto New Orleans to follow-up on a lead an ex-police detective I knew from my Jimmy Swaggart undercover investigation has unearthed. He has located a self-described "spirit man" who lives out on the Atchafalaya swamp. Apparently, this mystery man was once a writer from "up north" and after getting lost in the swamp more than twenty-five years earlier he had a spiritual awakening.

Exiting the Baton Rouge terminal, I stagger into the summer swelter and breath-taking humidity. I know this stifling sensation well after living here. Back then, the oppressive heat mixed with an equally potent anxiety created by my assignment. I was an imposter, a man living a big lie; someone who assumed a new name and identity to trick people; someone poking around in places where they had no business being. For six months I was undercover and ferreting out spiritual wrongdoing – and burdened with fear and anxiety of being discovered by some of the genuinely good people I ingratiated myself to.

Dialing up the air conditioner in my rental car, I motor through town with no destination in mind except to revisit my old haunts and let the muse have its way with me. This is my first time back in a long time, but it feels as if I never left. In fact, I have a nagging sensation that I left something behind here; some intimate piece of myself is waiting to be reunited.

After swinging by my old apartment on Sweetbriar Street, near the LSU campus (Louisiana State University),

I stop at Coffee Call and sit at my old table among Cajun regulars who play dominoes and linger over lattes and beignets. The conversation carries the beautiful distinctive tone and rambling cadence of southern Louisiana. Later, I drive the Old River Road, paralleling the Mississippi River and miles of sugar cane fields where mechanical harvesters churn up clouds of chaff. It hangs over the fields in a mist pervading the saturated air. The fragrance is sweet and mixes with the scent of the surrounding yellow pine forests, creating a unique bouquet. It is good to be here again.

I stop at Ashland Belle-Helene, a grand antebellum mansion deserted for nearly a hundred years. The grand old house has fallen into a sad and ruinous state. Walking along the overgrown driveway, the mansion's impressive, yet mournful colonnades stand like naked sentinels protecting its past greatness, and guarding against the encroachment of the forest and jungle-like vegetation. Not a speck of paint remains and the mansion seems to slump into itself. Three hundred years of moisture and interior rot has eaten away at its heart and soul.

The sun breaks through the mist and casts my shadow out in front of me. My shadow is the colonnade of my own fine house. While it appears strong and able, featuring wide, squared-off shoulders and a Roman facial silhouette, it is not what it appears to be. Like the stately colonnades of Ashland Belle-Helene, it is only aggrandizement, a strong facade hiding something diminished and lesser within.

The last time I visited this grand old dame, I was another person – both metaphorically and literally. Back then, the name I assumed was Randall Potts, my best childhood friend. I chose the name because Randall was my best friend from childhood. In 1977, Randall died mysteriously. We grew up together, lived in the same neighborhood and attended the same schools. I remember watching the classic film, Gone With The Wind, in his basement bedroom. Randall would have loved this grand old mansion. In a symbolic gesture, I borrowed his name to honor him and to keep his memory alive.

Back in Baton Rouge, I turn onto Blue Bonnet Boulevard and pull to the side of the road. From there, the road is wide and straight and I can see down a slight decline all the way Jimmy Swaggart's Assembly of God Church and religious campus. I sit quietly for a long time, trying to put everything into order, but the river of my thoughts are strong undercurrents and carry me away. What would the real Randall do if he were here? What advice might he offer?

I have regrets about this period and they wash up

against the shoals of my integrity and honor. I was gung-ho back then, wanting to make a name for myself by bringing down a lying, money-grubbing charlatan. Jimmy Swaggart preyed on people's trust, goodness and gullibility. He was one of the most powerful televangelists of his era, raking in hundreds of millions of dollars a year, ostensibly to help orphans in Central America, but diverting much of the cash to enrich himself and his cronies. In the morning he preached Christian family values, but after nightfall he cruised the sad side of New Orleans searching for the down-low with ten-dollar whores.

At the same time, I was a hypocrite too, lying and deceiving and masquerading as a lost soul, searching for answers. I told the good people of Swaggart's congregation that prior to arriving I had had a meaningless and superficial life. Then one day, in my darkest hour, a beam of pure light shone down on me from above and I had a spiritual awakening, a transformational experience. I told them I started listening to Reverend Swaggart on cable TV and decided to liquidate all my earthly goods and move to Baton Rouge, where I might be of service to the Lord and his people. Little did they or anyone know I was a spy, a plant sent by famed pornographer Larry Flynt, publisher of Hustler Magazine. My job was to ferret out the charlatan's wrongdoing and expose him.

I attended meetings, volunteered my time and ingratiated myself to everyone, telling ever bigger and more outlandish lies as I went. I couldn't stop myself really, and each new line of bullshit got more grandiose and preposterous. One night, after a single's group meeting, I walked a beautiful southern belle out to her car and told her my wife and children had been killed in a tragic fire and I felt responsible. I stood there blubbering like a baby. I realize now, I was truly a lost, tormented and pathetic soul.

In two short months, I ended up working as a volunteer on the same floor housing Swaggart's personal office. I gained the trust of his staff, and was privy to private, insider information. As others stood at the water cooler talking LSU football, I openly copied sensitive financial documents, and after hours one night planted a voice activated tape recorder in Swaggart's office.

Despite my deceit, his congregation embraced me openly, never questioning my motives or me. I met honest and lovely people and was taken aback by their acceptance of me. I'm not sure what I expected, but what I found was an open, educated and fairly prosperous group of people who appeared secure in themselves and their belief in God and salvation.

Pulling back on the roadway, I hit the accelerator and fly by Swaggart's church and bible college at more than fifty miles an hour. At the intersection of Blue Bonnet and Perkins Road, I flip a U-turn and drive by again – this time slower.

Something is happening in the chapel and the parking lot is filling up with cars. Without thinking I pull into the parking lot and join a group walking toward the entrance. They are sparkling clean and dressed in Sunday finest. Some carry beautifully wrapped gifts. The women are wearing designer labels and the men are in conservative slacks, dress shirts and ties. A man nods in my direction and I nod back.

Despite Swaggart's disgrace over the infamous Debra McMurphre sex scandal and his now famous, "I have sinned," sound bite, today he is back in the pulpit and one of the richest men in Louisiana. He is the largest private landlord in the state, owning hundreds of houses and commercial properties. During my investigation, he was the most powerful man in the state and known to carry grudges. Had he known I was sent by the devil, Larry Flynt, to expose him, I would have ended up down on the bayou, a late night snack for the gators.

Stepping across the threshold into Swaggart's church,

once again I feel a mix of comfort, anxiety and fear. So much fear, in fact, I feel as if the floor is moving under my feet. What if Swaggart is standing inside the foyer and recognizes me? After all, the media splashed my face across TV screens and in newspapers once the story broke.

A year after his downfall, I was back in New Orleans covering a lawsuit against him. I was in the men's room at the New Orleans courthouse standing at a urinal when someone saddled up next to me at the adjacent bowl. The man stared at me until it became uncomfortable, so I turned to face him. It was Jimmy Swaggart. A smile flushed across his oversized, fleshy face, "I know who you are," he announced smiling and proud of himself. "I recognize you."

"I know who you are, too!" I snapped back, pulling myself back in and zipping my trousers closed. Turning to leave, I felt warm water running down both legs and realized I hadn't finished the job I was there to accomplish. As the restroom door closed behind me, I heard Jimmy humming a few haunting bars from what sounded like a sad church hymn.

Back inside his church, Swaggart is nowhere in sight and I briefly got caught-up in a wedding celebration for a smart-looking young couple. Despite not knowing a soul and having a bitter taste in my mouth over my own failed marriage, I feel oddly comfortable and happy to wish this beautiful couple good luck. For a few weird moments, I was outside myself and home again – a member of a loving family once more.

By the time the wedding ceremony concluded, I had been invited by the mother of the bride – a beautiful divorcee - to the reception at the Swaggart family compound a mile or two away. With a southern gentlemen's measured grace, I took her hand into mine, bowed from the waist, thanked her warmly and declined.

Afterward, I drove to the Rural Life Museum, a place I found sanctuary during the long months living alone in the capitol city. There among hundreds of acres of plowed but mostly fallow fields, I walked a single-track road from one end of the historic farm to the other almost daily for months. It was a place to brood and contemplate; a place to let anxieties and fears find a voice.

What I enjoyed most but struck me as odd at the time was that the place was always empty. Despite being surrounded by the city and possessing a dreamy, timeless natural environment that city dwellers so appreciate, I can't remember seeing another person there. After a few weeks, it became my private park, a buffer zone between the real and unreal life I led.

On this day, I park my rental near the back entrance and stroll a leaf-strewn country lane to an old wooden bridge that crosses a little used waterway and then continues onto the museum's grounds. The surrounding flora and fauna create a sense of cloister and protection. It's strange how our minds work, how details and peripheral objects of a place disappear until the moment we see them again. Years later when we see these details and objects they instantly come alive, returning to the forefront of our consciousness to take a bow, as if to say we've always been right here waiting.

Tucked away across a plowed field is my favorite place here, a lush botanical garden. It's an inner sanctum of overgrown mazes populated by flowerbeds and trees and birds and marble statues and moss-covered monuments. Everything has the look of age and beautiful disrepair, like the cemeteries we cherish but do not visit often. I will save this garden for last. On my left is a recreation of a nineteenth century southern town's main street. All the buildings are authentic but were moved here from different locations. All totaled there are maybe ten buildings including a store, a blacksmith shop and a one-room schoolhouse.

I meander the long narrow dirt road that runs

through the center of the farm, lined by neatly furrowed fields, consumed with memories of my many walks here. My thoughts carry me back to my dear friend Randall Potts. Looking back it is easy to see that Randall was deeper and further advanced intellectually and spiritually than I was during those heady high school days. As teenagers we often slept out in my backyard and spent dreamy summer nights laying on the grass watching for shooting stars. I talked about girls and parties while Randall had theories about science, evolution, politics, and especially the size and complexity of the cosmos.

In September of 1963 we stood cheek by jowl with hundreds of others and shook the hand of our ill-fated hero, President John F. Kennedy, just weeks before he was slain in Dallas. We sobbed in each other's arms the day he died. By the end of that corpulent decade, I was a college activist, speaking out against the war in Vietnam and following the mantra of the cultural moment: Tune-in, Turn-on and Drop-out. Randall followed another path, a contemplative one. He journeyed the fifth direction, the one that goes from the outside to the inside. He traveled to India and then to Spain to study Transcendental Meditation (TM) at the feet of the Maharishi Mahesh Yogi. Even as I descended into a personal hell of mistakes and drugs, he ascended to become an enlightened soul, teaching TM and running a meditation center, our friendship stayed strong and enduring.

Our last face-to-face meeting has troubled me for years. It left me with questions I can never answer. It happened one cold February morning as I was sitting at the counter of the Pinecone, a popular restaurant when someone tapped me on the shoulder. It was Randall. I hadn't seen him in a few months because I had been living in Colorado and had just gotten into town a few days earlier. After a warm greeting, Randall told me he knew I was going to be there that morning and needed to talk to me.

The problem was there was no way he could have known I was going to be there that morning because I didn't know myself. The only reason I was even in the neighborhood was because I had a toothache the night before and made an emergency appointment with a dentist whose office is in the area. Afterward, as I walked to my car, I made a snap decision to slip into the Pinecone for a cup of coffee. It was the first time I'd set foot inside the Pinecone for many years. Our meeting was purely coincidental, yet he maintained he knew I would be there.

When I asked him about this, he just repeated himself, telling me he knew I would be there and he needed to talk to me.

We moved to a back booth where in high school we sat and smoked cigarettes and Randall told me a fantastic story. He was excited and animated and told me he was on the verge of learning the truth about never-ending life. I can still see his handsome face and the way his eyelashes fluttered when he was saying something important. Never-ending life, I wondered? I was amazed and incredulous and sat there quietly and listened. Despite what he was telling me, he seemed perfectly lucid, articulate and in command. He said the truth about never-ending life would be delivered to mankind sometime in the future, but he wasn't sure when. He was certain, however, that this truth would be delivered through music.

When I asked how he knew this, he admitted it came to him during meditation. He had been meditating more than ten hours a day and practicing a powerful form of meditation called Kundilini, which I had never heard of. He explained the Kundilini process by saying you inhale and exhale oxygen quickly over and over again to the point of hyperventilation, and then exhale completely and hold your breath. He confided that because of the number of hours he devoted to meditating, he was experiencing some mental health problems and was even hallucinating like the times we took LSD. He said it was not uncommon for people who meditated so many hours to have similar side effects. He admitted he had lost touch with reality a few months earlier and spent a week in a psychiatric hospital. I was concerned and told him so.

When we parted, we embraced and I invited him to my new apartment for dinner the next week. Then Randall did something I will never forget, he looked into my eyes and said,

"I've never told you this, but I want to thank you for being my friend. When we were kids I had no real friends. You took me in and opened your heart to me. You taught me how to talk to people and introduced me to everyone as your best friend. I don't know what I would have done without you, Mark. I can't thank you enough for that."

I remember feeling embarrassed and thinking it was unusual, but it felt good and I was honored and pleased. At home, I wrote everything he said into my journal so I would not forget any of it. I called our mutual friend, Robin Johnson, and told him what transpired.

On the day we were to have dinner, I got a call from his mother and she told me Randall had died the night before while meditating. He was found sitting against a wall in the lotus position. Randall was twenty-seven-years old.

The autopsy report found nothing wrong with him, except there was no oxygen in his lungs or blood stream. After carrying his coffin to the gravesite, his mother handed me an article about other members of TM who had died in a similar way.

Randall intentionally exhaled the oxygen from his lungs and transcended off this mortal coil. He learned the truth about never-ending life and his transformation was complete.

Much later I came to understand that during our last meeting, Randall was telling me goodbye. I only wish I had understood that back then. I've been trying to tell my beloved friend Randall goodbye ever since.

THE ATCHAFALAYA BASIN

Plop. Splash.

Something from above, coming from a stand of wild pecan trees growing out over the bayou, just dropped into the calm water a few feet away. The sound is deep and throaty as if the water only reluctantly opened to swallow the object, and once it did, it closed up quickly, sealing the breach with a splash. We have been sitting motionless here in a canoe for nearly a half hour, listening to the swamp. I trace the trajectory of the mystery object from its ever-widening concentric rings on the water's surface to an overhanging branch above where a large, red squirrel sits looking down at us.

"Dun't want us here," Lawrence says flatly. "Swamp dun't want us either – better off without us."

Lawrence speaks with a clipped Acadian accent. It is the first thing he has said in nearly an hour. He is taking me to his place out in the Atchafalaya basin. He wants to show me the place so I can get a better idea of the transformation that occurred out here. I have the feeling he is taking me on the scenic route, the long way around.

"The swamp wants nothing from us, 'cept maybe for us to be real, something we've forgotten how to be," he shoots a glance at me. Do I get his gist? "Wants us to show our true nature."

"Seems fair enough," I whisper.

Around these parts, Lawrence is a swamp philosopher, someone who has been out on the basin for so long people listen to him as if he might have something important to say.

"Not meaning to be impolite," Lawrence looks away, "but most people don't know a damn thing 'bout who they are, or 'bout their nature."

"I suspect you are right," I answer. "I don't know much

about my *true nature* either, except it's probably worth airing out a little."

"People come down to the swamp thinkin' its Disneyland. Like old Walt Disney designed it his-self just for them. They're waitin' for a gator to jump outta the water at 'em, or a snake to drop inta' the boat so they can tell their friends back home 'bout it."

As Lawrence talks, the squirrel moves along the branch and disappears into a cluster of leaves, calkin and dark brown pecans.

"People come down around these parts thinkin' that man is the boss – the God of it all – but it ain't true. Swamp holds the power."

Lawrence opens his arms out and upward, "It's what it is - what it's always been."

I nod in agreement, amazed at the beauty and silence.

"If we left right now and never came back, the swamp wouldn't give a damn. It'd continue on, just as it is now. Perfect."

Lawrence pulls the fingers of both hands through his long, sweat-soaked, salt-and-pepper hair from front to back, then tucks it behind his ears. "You're a writer, huh? Know anything about allegory?"

"Some."

"This here swamp is an allegory to the complexity of man – and *the wonder* man can't accept about his self." Lawrence sits up straight and blinks as if waiting for me to reply, then tilts his head from side to side like a rare bird.

I say nothing, but I'm thinking Lawrence is about the same height, weight and about the same age as Dave Thomson. I try to overlay my memory of Dave's photographs on Lawrence to see if it might be a match.

"There are waterways and inlets and islands and lagoons and marshes that bubble up and meet the ocean at places that are neither land nor water. The inside of a man is like that, too. Can't be separated out; no one knows where it starts or where it ends."

"Nice," I remark, thinking how he sounds less homegrown Cajun and more northern intellectual. A writer.

"Just like us, the swamp's fragrances can be sweet and delicious or it can bubble up from below, a sewer of rot and reek, a stench that takes your breath away; a stinking bile so nasty it'll burn right on through you."

The squirrel appears out of the cluster with a pecan and moves along the branch to position itself above the canoe. Its stubby arms and hands struggle with the pecan, but its big red bushy tail is at ease, undulating back and forth and reminding me of my Turkish Angora cat, Whitestuff, back home.

Lawrence leans forward and confides, "If we would be quiet for just a minute and stop our own internal jabberwocky, we'd be more like the swamp. The secret is to stop running our mental mouth."

I place my thumb and forefinger together and zip my forehead shut.

"Out here we're not big shots," he shakes his head. "People can't stand that idea."

"You've thought a good deal about this . . ."

"Livin' out in nature, you consider your *own* nature more than most – more than you can in a city."

"You lived in the city?"

"I've lived in cities."

"You're not from here, are you? I mean, Louisiana?"

Lawrence stiffens. Without answering, he takes the boat's oars in his big, dirty hands and in one beautifully efficient and powerful stroke, launches us across the water. Just as we depart, something hits me atop the head. Looking up, I see the squirrel staring down, its tail now an explanation point. At the bottom of the canoe is a big golden pecan.

After some hard and powerful rowing, going from one inlet to an outlet and then down an overgrown passageway, we end up in a cyprus tree-lined alleyway. Lawrence lets us glide across a quiet stretch of water bordered by a sandy shoreline where some mature alligators sun themselves.

"Dun't really matter where I came from," Lawrence announces, "or how I came here."

After more meandering – going around and around as far as I can tell – we enter an overgrown passageway just wide enough for the canoe to negotiate. It is blocked at the far end by a profusion of overhanging branches, downed tree limbs and a bramble of vines with magnolia-like red and white fluted flowers. At its end, Lawrence uses an oar to pull back a curtain of foliage to expose a circular shaped, clear water lagoon surrounded by giant old-growth oak trees. A picturesque Cajun shack with a boat dock sits on its far side near the base of several trees.

I feel as if I have been transported away to some never-neverland.

The lagoon and house are hidden and protected by the oaks that stretch their Spanish Moss laden limbs up and out, almost interlocking at the center and creating a lush canopy of shade below. The scene is perfect and unreal, and for an instant nature cracks open the doorway to the possibilities we only know as children.

I now know why Lawrence wanted me to see this

place.

"It's somethin, in't?" he mutters.

"Amazing," I respond.

Lawrence shoots a good-natured smile and I see Dave Thomson.

"I never really leave this place," he says, "even when I'm gone."

The small three-room house is old, leans to one side and has no electricity, running water or toilet. It sits half on land and half on stilts at the water's edge. The boat dock doubles as the front porch and we disembark. Lawrence moves a broken-down patio chair to the center of the porch and invites me to sit down. He goes about his work, retrieving a submerged trap secured to the dock with a chain to reveal a crawdad-laden treasure. I am happy just to sit and marvel at this magical environment, and Lawrence disappears into the kitchen. Soon, the delicious aroma of red beans, rice and steaming crawdads fills the air.

To the south, a vast cyprus forest stands in the swamp water and recedes into the distance until it disappears. Its beauty is mysterious, defying explanation or unraveling. To the south and west, a tropical mangrove and pineland forest stretches out to meet the Gulf of Mexico some miles away. A breeze carries a mixture of fragrances, Cajun delicacies, exotic flowers, salt water and the deep, rich organic smell that is rotting earth.

After a splendid dinner sucking crawdads dipped in Lawrence's special hot sauce of wild peppers and herbs collected nearby, he retrieves a bottle of homemade red wine and sits Indian style on the porch next to me. He narrates the story of the house and property.

The land was homesteaded more than three hundred years ago by a French Acadian family who came from Canada and stumbled on the location after Indians told them there was good hunting nearby. They planted the oaks the year they arrived. They wanted to farm, but gave up on that idea and fished, hunted and harvested pecans that they traded for goods at the store in Boudrow. According to Lawrence, there was no need to work. Except for an occasional heavy storm or hurricane, living off the abundant land was easy. All they had to do was drop a fishing line in the water for fresh or salt-water fish. They hunted white tail deer, wild boar, turkey, duck and squirrel. Many kinds of nuts and fruits were in abundance. The family members were accomplished musicians and distillers of special liquors and malt whiskey. As far as he knew, no one owned the land and the last of the original family died more than forty years ago.

"I found the place by accident after living on the streets in Nawlins and then hitching a ride north with a guy who lives in up in Sidell.

"We argued and he dropped me off out on the high-way," Lawrence nodded to the north. "I was pretty much down and out and decided to end it all, so I just hiked off cross-country and got lost." He shook his head, "It was a stupid, but I didn't care. After a day or two I stumbled onto the place. I saw the oaks from a distance and thought I could climb one to get a look around.

"I knew right away this was the place. It took about a year to fix it up, and I collected cans and took odd jobs for building materials."

"I was told you were a hermit," I added. "That you'd show up in town and instead of talking, you sort-of grunt-ed."

"Well, damn. That's about right. I didn't want to tell anyone where I was living, worried they'd run me off, and so I spent most of a decade hiding out here. Didn't have one visitor; didn't really have the inclination to talk to any one either."

"What happened? What changed?"

"Look around. This is what happened." He motions around him. "I fell in love with the place and wanted nothing more than just to stay put. Lost track of days and weeks and my only calendar was the sun, waterways and pecan trees."

"Something must have happened."

"Nature does something to you…"

I understood what Lawrence was saying but asked, "Why did you start going to town?"

"Well, I've always been a reader so I started borrowing books from the library over in Boudrow. The only thing they knew about me was I wasn't one of them, and I came out of the swamp. Guess I got a reputation. I returned every one of those books.

"One day, an old gal at the library asked what I was reading and we started talking. Just sort-of took off after that."

I saw my opportunity, "You like to read?"

"I read once that a good library makes an excellent father."

"You write, too?"

"I do a little writing, guess you might say." He turns his head to the house, and changes the subject. "Not meaning to be nosy, but what 'cha doin' in these parts?"

"I'm looking for a guy by the name of David Thomson. He is a writer, like me."

"Uh huh," Lawrence said, tilting his head to the left. "People tell me you think I might be him."

It is dark now and the stars glint through the canopy above, creating an eerie light show.

"I'm hoping you might be," I say, suddenly feeling anxious. Here I am out in the middle of the biggest swamp in America with a man I just met a few hours ago. For all I know, Lawrence might be unbalanced and dangerous. "I've been looking for him for a long time now.

"Just left his sister, Emme, a couple days ago. She's heartbroken." I watch to gauge his reaction. He shifts from one bun to the other and then gets to his knees.

"The family has been waiting for Dave to come home for years." I continue, "It's been a long time."

"How long?"

"August of '79."

"He's dead," Lawrence announces, matter-of-factly.

"That's what I thought too, but now I don't know. People disappear and then pop up all the time. It's more common than you think."

"What business is it of yours?"

"I like mysteries."

"So, you think I am this Dave?"

"Are you?"

"That's what Derek says, you think I might be him."

Silence.

Lawrence sits back down, and turns his back to me. "What if I were this David Thomson? What then?"

"Don't know."

"Guess you'd have to find another mystery."

Laughter.

"If I were him, would you try to convince me to leave the only life that has ever given me a moment's peace for one I rejected and was unhappy with?"

"How do you know Dave was unhappy?"

"Don't. Something made him go."

"He was heartbroken over his brother's death and disillusioned about things."

"Do I look heartbroken?"

"That was a long time ago. What about back then?"

"I've had my share of death and heartbreak. You can't live without having it fall on your shoulders. And you know, in a way, it brought me to this place – via a highway of alcohol, drugs and insanity. "

Lawrence struggles to control his emotions.

"Look, I don't know anything about Dave Thomson," he explains. "I left my other life thirty years ago and I am no longer that person. I'm not telling you or anyone else more than that. I am the man you see and no one else. The metamorphosis that brought me to this place is complete. There are no shadows standing behind me."

Lawrence's voice changes and has a new timber; the wise man is now speaking. Turning back to face me, he goes on,

"Most people go their entire lives and never find the real person living inside. It usually takes some powerful force like nature or the death of a loved one to give us the opportunity to see who we truly are and not who we would like to be, or who others want us to be. We need to court unpopularity to find ourselves. It won't happen jumping through hoops for people who really do not care about us, but who judge us and rule our lives.

"One way to find yourself is to go into the wild. Nature doesn't care what you wear or whether you comb your hair or take a bath. It doesn't care who you voted for or what church you belong to, or how much money you have in the bank or what kind of car you drive or whether your house is a mansion or shack. Nature accepts us for who we are, mankind does not."

Lawrence fills my glass again, "Look around," he motions with his head, "God's cathedral! This is the greatest church ever conceived.

"I read once that the grand cathedrals of Europe, those huge caverns with high ceilings a hundred feet up, were designed to mimic caves where the first Christians were forced to hide and practice Christianity in secret.

"Something about nature, its size, simplicity and power, makes us whole. I'm living proof. It doesn't care if we are sinners or losers or alcoholics or drug addicts. Out here, there is no judgment, no one looking over your shoulder, *every thing* is good and worthy of celebrating and sharing."

We sit quietly for a long time, enjoying the sounds of the night. Lawrence smokes hand rolled cigarettes, and after a while offers me a sleeping mat he rolled out in his living room. He says he is going to sit up and take in the night.

At dawn, an eerie fog lays in the cypress swamp, hovering above the water's surface in the middle ground, and below the tops of the trees. It collects around the Spanish moss in the branches and recedes deep into the forest where it mists away the horizon.

Lawrence is gone, slipping away during the night. His canoe is gone, too.

At first, I think little of Lawrence's absence, concluding he is doing swamp things, collecting nuts or berries or fishing for breakfast, but few hours later, I know he is not coming back. He left me alone on purpose, to discover the power of this natural place for myself. If I want to know him better, to know what motivates him, to discover what keeps him here and feeling so in-tune, I can learn more from his absence than his presence.

Still, I wait until late mid-morning before venturing out behind the house to wander through the pine forest, with no destination in mind. I let a trail of mushrooms and swamp mallow and ribbon snakes and green tree frogs and fabulous purple wild violets and hanging orange iris pick my path. As I move from one place to the next, the pine-land is pocked with deep clear pools of fresh water where turtles float effortlessly and foot-long alligators sun them-selves; where huge, luminescent, blue-winged dragon flies and damsel flies feast on over-ripened passion fruit and sweet fleabane.

It is the dry season and the land that is normally an impenetrable mangrove of submerged roots and vines, is dried-out and easily navigable. At its edges are wet marsh-lands where snowy egrets and blue and green herons stalk the water's edge on long spindly legs. They hunt mussels and snails and snakes and insects. Gold and red crested woods ducks and dark coots and spotted sandpipers float nearby on the water's reflective surface. Above, savannah sparrows and cedar waxwings and brown thrashers race between pine tree shafts, talking loudly and playing kamikaze games.

The oaks surrounding the shack are my reference point and I keep them in sight as long as I can before losing them at the horizon. I've spent years hiking the Rockies and the sandstone canyons of the southwest and have developed a fairly keen internal compass. I am never really fearful I will lose my way, ultimately knowing I am on a small inlet of land and will find my way back no matter what direction I proceed. At my furthest point, I suspect I am no more than a mile from where I started.

In the early afternoon I find myself at the center of a large field of waist-high salt grass and decide to lay in it – to become part of this magnificent slice of nature, to feel how it might feel to be *it*. Lying in the long grass reminds me of Herman Hesse's book, *Siddhartha*. This is not the first time I have tried, with some success, to merge with the earth and all that call it home. In his book, Hesse's Siddhartha is a seeker of truth and his spiritual quest includes wandering nature and attempting to become part of it.

Lying there in the deep grass, I am warm, comfortable and at peace. The tall, straight stalks of grass shimmer with a gold-green light and move in concert as the wind wafts them back and forth or round and round. Winged insects, on their way from one place to another, buzz by and fill the silence with their beating wings. I am no longer at the center of the universe and little more than a bit player. I am dizzy. I am not the god-like entity I believed myself to be. I am part of nature, not the *Lord* of it. I am a small - but not insignificant – part of it. For these few fleeting moments, I am my true self, a part of nature, not apart from it.

I remember Siddhartha's dilemma: the attempt to lose himself so he might discover a greater truth about life. But Siddhartha's problem, and mine, is *self*.

It is the *self* I need to free myself from. Why am I not able to overcome it? No other thing in this world has kept my thoughts as busy as my own *self*. It started early-on when I was a boy, this mystery of me being alive; of me being the one and the only; of me being at the center of the universe; of me being separated and isolated from all other things; of me being special! And, these thoughts always lead back to the beginning and the realization that there is nothing I truly know less about than myself.

For a few minutes in the tall grass, I am free of *self* and my species' need to control the nature of everything. I am liberated and light, as if I might vaporize and float away.

Later, back at the house, I am happy to find Lawrence has not returned. I nap on the porch in the shade and then attempt, without success, to duplicate the delicious rice and red beans he prepared. I look around for the thick folder of papers I had seen the night before, and assumed contained his writings, but it is missing.

I remember something Lawrence mentioned the night before, 'the road is that way,' he said, nodding to the north. Behind the house, I find a hammer and an old coffee can filled with big nails. Pulling two aging two-by-four studs from a rotting pile of wood I use a hand saw to cut them into rungs, then one by one, nail them to the trunk of an oak, creating a ladder up to a huge branch where I can climb even higher.

From my vantage point, it appears the swamp continues unbroken in all directions. I did, however, hear an automobile earlier and it seemed closer than I would have suspected. I also remember hearing a car in the distance as we neared the secret grotto yesterday. The road is out there and probably closer than Lawrence wants me to believe.

There are still a few hours of daylight so I decide to investigate. Working my way around the other side of the lagoon where we came in, I swim or wade in an easterly direction for about half an hour before turning back. The water is deep and I feel claustrophobic because of the thick overgrowth and the idea of bloodsuckers, snakes and alligators doesn't help either. Several times I am forced to back track, but unlike earlier in the day, I make sure I can see the oak trees to the west. After several attempts at moving directly east, I turn north to find the marsh gives way to the same kind of dried mangrove I hiked earlier in the day. A sparse pine forest soon turns into a stand of giant ferns, making it difficult to proceed and impossible to see more than a few feet ahead or behind. I fight through bouts of panic by concentrating on just pushing forward. After about fifteen minutes, I pull a large fern frond back to discover the dead-end dirt road I drove in on.

Twenty minutes later, I am standing at my rental car. In the distance, perhaps a thousand yards away, I can see the tops of the mighty oak trees. Lawrence's secret Atchafalaya paradise is only a ten-minute canoe trip from the end of the road.

CHAPTER TWENTY-FIVE

RIO VERDE

MAY 2020

CHEMO BUT ALIVE

The six-month chemo regime is over and I should be happy, but there's not much left of me to celebrate. So far, the aftermath is as bad as the treatments. My oncologist reports that recent scans miraculously show the tumors on my spinal column are gone – kaputski – and the random circulating cancer cells have ostensibly been exterminated. Yet I haven't so much dodged a bullet as I've been hit directly by it. The general chemo damage is system wide, substantial and profound in implication. It might be analogous to carpet-bombing. Hit everything hard, destroy it all and hope you eliminate the target.

Medically speaking, I'm in remission. There is no cure for metastatic prostate cancer. Now months later, I'm still sick from the chemical poisoning and I'm not getting any better, I'm actually getting worse. This damage is permanent. Not only am I a victim of prostate cancer, but now I have a multitude of new serious health problems created by the chemical onslaught.

I've been through this before and should have known better. How did I let this happen?

Years ago I helped my best friend Nancy as she valiantly fought a losing battle against liver cancer. She had so much to live for: the mother of three with one a pre-teen, a grad school graduate who was devoted to her special needs students, a daughter who cared for her aging parents and a force of nature who served up love, laughter and lasagna to her large cadre of friends and loved ones. Nancy fought hard, suffered enormously and she willingly underwent nearly every new treatment doctors came up with. I once warned her, "For every upside a promising treatment may offer, there are down sides and the chance it (the treatment) could make things worse."

Ultimately, it was her fighting nature and decision to undergo unproven treatments that was her undoing. Was she going to die anyway? Yes, but her manic search for an escape route led from one setback to another. Liver cancer is extraordinarily painful and in an attempt to mitigate this pain she followed a well-meaning doctor's advice to try a new experimental technique of severing pain nerves at the spinal column and leading to her liver. Regrettably, the doctor cut the wrong nerves and instead severed those leading to her digestive track. This left her unable to assimilate nutrients from digesting food. Had she declined this treatment, the fabulous personage she was and had always been would have survived until the cancer killed her. As it was, she was transformed into a non-verbal starving zombie-like shell, dazed by excruciating pain and absent the sparkle, spirit and fire that so characterized the totality of her life.

Now, my decision to undergo chemotherapy has robbed me too of the dynamic and passionate man I believe I've always been. The corrosive chemicals brought me to my knees and permanently damaged my digestive, neurological and skeletal systems. Before chemo I was proud of my near perfect posture, a product of being a modern dancer in my twenties. At six foot two inches tall, I received compliments over the years on how I carried myself. When I get out of bed in the morning now, I resemble a picture I once saw of an old Jewish man being beaten by Nazi grey shirts in the streets of Berlin in the mid-1930s. He was bent and broken. And that is how I feel – bent and broken. It takes a few minutes now to stand straight up, to stack one vertebrae atop the next until I am erect. Today, every bone in my skeleton aches. I had no conception of aching bones before chemo.

I am now a fall risk. A one-time talented athlete and modern dancer I am unable to pass a simple field sobriety test. I can no longer walk a straight line. If the light is low indoors or I walk outside at night I simply fall over. These falls are serious, like the one that ended in broken ribs, a collapsed lung, a damaged heart and a week's hospitalization at the Mayo Clinic. Chemo did this to me. My feet are perpetually frozen with a burning numbness. I can no longer make a fist without severe pain. The joints in my hands are extremely sensitive and I've developed trigger or flip finger – the painful inability to open my fingers from a closed or semi-closed position. I am now forced to take strong pain meds to fight constant and debilitating bone pain in my femurs, hips, feet, hands, shoulders and back. I have constant and ongoing nausea, dizziness and irritable bowel syndrome.

My cognitive and creative functions have been impacted, too. Writers use the top five percent of their neurological abilities to make a living. A keen intellect and the refined ability to quickly analyze materials are basic and essential requirements. Since chemo I sometimes struggle for the right word or find it difficult to maintain my concentration during long work periods. This is devastating psychologically and combines with the fuzziness chemo is famous for and leads to immense frustration and bouts of irritability.

After months of denials my oncologist admitted that these and other conditions I now suffer from were caused by the months of chemotherapy. The technical term for this damage is neuropathy, the permanent damage to the nervous system and to many of the functions it oversees.

Of all my new disabilities, the worst is the unforgiving and ever-present fatigue. Some days I sleep twelve hours and get up exhausted. On good days, I have a two-to-four hour window of modest energy. I can pick one physical activity a day – say going for a short walk with my pups around the neighborhood. I've harnessed my willpower to fight this fatigue, only to be defeated again and again. This fatigue is organic and will not be moved by my cosmic, psychic and metaphysical strength. Writers need long blocks of uninterrupted time to work, so my productivity suffers greatly. With or without disabilities, writing is hard work. Albert Einstein once said that writing is the hardest work of all. As proof, he said, "Look around, how many people do you see doing it?"

Was chemotherapy worth it? No. I acknowledge that the brutal and inhumane treatments have kept me alive. I could not sit here and write this if I were dead. Yes, I'm alive but just barely living. Like my dynamic friend Nancy, the life that was once mine and the person I once was are now gone. But here I am today; bent over at my writing desk, pretending that this is enough because it is all I have.

Would I recommend chemotherapy? Yes, but with this caveat: You must be young, your cancer must be in a beginning stage, and chemotherapy must offer a chance for a total cure. However, if you have a terminal diagnosis, are over the age of fifty, and if the treatments only offer low quality added time, I strongly advise against it. Relish the time you have left. Be *you* - the person you've always been – and live your life to its natural end. We all die.

Duel Consciousness

I've spent the last 18 months knowing I was going to die of cancer. I consider my demise daily and assumed I'd be long gone by now. My status will change soon enough, but until then I'm reminded of my fate by the devastating problems related to my disease and its treatments. At some point I found myself telling friends and family that I am mostly at peace with the idea of dying, but I have no idea how to live – in the present.

One of the greatest challenges has been learning how to live in the present moment while simultaneously and consciously making provisions for my own death.

How can I enjoy thinking about attending the Paul McCartney concert next year when next year may never arrive? How do I respond to Lana when she wants to plan a dream trip to Italy when the first thought to pop into my head is, how am I going to do that, I am dying?

Living with cancer has a ruinous effect on perceptions, calculations, decisions, plans, opportunities and each overt attempt to maintain some semblance of satisfaction, fulfillment or contentment with life. The drawbacks of living in the present with its corrosive dread about a canceled future are devastating. The sustaining substance of everyday living is leached away by visions of gruesome disabilities, infirmity and loss. These issues are so fundamental and perplexing, it took a year for me to conclude it was impossible to best this problem and I would need to look elsewhere for a reasoned answer.

I tried writing about it, hoping the process of this work would somehow sift through the superfluous and terrifying to leave behind a refined essence or understanding I could employ to move forward in a positive and life affirming way. But the result was more confusion.

I asked those in a similar situation how they remained positive. I read books and essays about dying. I lost myself in Julie Yip-Williams' book, *The Unwinding of a Miracle* and read between the lines of Elaine Pagels', award winning, *Why Religion?* even though I already concluded religion serves only itself. With each new attempt or personal experience I felt I *was* getting closer to seeing an outline or silhouette of a possible solution.

But it wasn't until July of 2019, when I read an essay, *Living Intimately with Thoughts of Death*, by Susan Gubar, that the missing puzzle parts started coming together for me. She has been fighting ovarian cancer for a decade. Gubar writes, "Since my cancer diagnosis, I have lived intimately with thoughts of death. Cancer patients of all ages and stages, as well as people with other ruinous conditions often experience a double frame of mind." She writes that introspection about this state of mind may be the most important work we can undertake.

She goes on to say that a double frame of mind helped equip imperiled patients to evolve a new and intoxicating clarification of their human condition. She used W.E.B. Dubois, the famed African American writer and civil rights activist, who coined a phrase "double consciousness" as an example to explain how blacks growing up in America with its discrimination and abuse can simultaneously live constructively and in harmony with themselves and society.

It was like a bolt of lightning. Suddenly I had the answer. One consciousness to serve the life I had always known, and a second, separate consciousness to contemplate the ideas and views of my new imperiled existence. These two consciousnesses have silenced the contradictory voices by separating them into individual and equal arenas.

Chapter Twenty-Six

Rio Verde

June 2020

Welcome Home

I am awakened by a sound that fades in and out so I sit up in the darkened bedroom on the edge of the bed. Sometimes the sound is almost discernable and I think loud voices are coming from somewhere outside. Other times I'm convinced it's part of the tinnitus I suffer from. If Lana were here she could tell me if it is real or the random misfirings of my brain. After the months of heavy chemo and a host of other ailments related to it or my condition, my thoughts are sometimes muddled and my analytical abilities are impaired.

After a few minutes I move slowly outside on the front porch. Sounds travel long distances in the Sonoran Desert and there are times I can hear the neighbors talking a quarter mile away. From the porch I hear dogs barking, women laughing or crying and men shouting. These sounds float in on the breeze and for an instant they are crystal clear, then just as quickly they become garbled and indistinguishable. Back inside I find Pierre and Ava undisturbed in a deep sleep. These beautiful pups are our early warning system and usually alert us to any outside sounds.

I slip my shoes on, grab a flashlight and saunter off in the direction of the sounds in the moonless night. A block or so away I can clearly hear laughing now and someone shouting my name. It's coming from the McDowell Nature Preserve to the west. This makes no sense for a number of reasons. First, it's 3 a.m. and highly unlikely anyone is out partying where no roads or trails exist. Secondly, it's preposterous to think someone is calling out to me, and thirdly, the entire idea is just insane.

Trying to get closer, I walk up the long driveway of a large expensive winter home to the backyard. The house is closed up for the blistering summer and I stand at the fence line abutting the preserve. Out in the blackness I spot a wildly flickering light coming from what must be a large campfire. The light dances off a nearby hill and a stand of tall saguaro close by. Someone is singing boisterously now and while I can't really make anything out, I see silhouettes moving about, they are cast out like grotesque figures in the firelight.

Meanwhile, I entertain the idea that all of this is an elaborate dream and I'm not really watching some ludicrous gathering out in the desert with people calling my name, but I'm at home asleep in my bed. I pinch myself and it hurts. After a half hour or so of watching and listening I decide to get more comfortable by sitting on the patio of the house near the swimming pool. Turning to face the house and pool, suddenly a line of colorful patio lights flash on and standing there with drinks in their hands and party hats on their heads are Mick Tripp and Nancy Delafara and Randall Potts and Sylvia Knight and Dina Bassett and Leslie Majors and Bud Mixon and Phil Sullivan and Robin Johnson and Wendy Wood. There are other people there too, but I can't make out who they are. Cheers go up and shouts of congratulations fill the silent desert night. A lifetime's worth of confidants and lovers and fellow travelers and best friends – all who happen to be dead – are standing there smiling, laughing and celebrating me.

"SURPRISE!" they holler in unison and sing out,

"WELCOME TO THE CAPITAL OF PARADISE!"

CPSIA information can be obtained
at www.ICGtesting.com
Printed in the USA
FSHW012154090921
84596FS